GEORGIALINA

Wille Morris might well have written, "Just as our parents and grandparents did, we rock on the front porch and recall old times as lightning bugs fire up and heat lightning glows on the horizon."

PHOTOGRAPH BY ROBERT C. CLARK.

Georgialina

 **A SOUTHLAND
AS WE KNEW IT**

Tom Poland

The University of South Carolina Press

© 2015 University of South Carolina

Published by the University of South Carolina Press
Columbia, South Carolina 29208

www.sc.edu/uscpress

Manufactured in the United States of America

24 23 22 21 20 19 18 17 16 15
10 9 8 7 6 5 4 3 2 1

Library of Congress Cataloging-in-Publication Data
can be found at http://catalog.loc.gov/.

ISBN: 978-1-61117-594-3 (paperback)
ISBN: 978-1-61117-595-0 (ebook)

Original versions of the columns, features, and essays in *Georgialina:
A Southland as We Knew It* first appeared in the following publications:
*Like the Dew: A Journal of Southern Culture and Politics; Blythewood Leader;
Lincoln Journal* (Lincolnton, Georgia); *McCormick Messenger; Midlands Life;
Midlands Biz; Sandlapper; South Carolina Wildlife;* and *Smiles Magazine.*

This book was printed on recycled paper with
30 percent postconsumer waste content.

For Mom, who faithfully clipped and saved every column . . .
even the ones she didn't like

Where Georgialina Began

The Classic South . . . Lincoln County, Georgia, backcountry

Where Georgialina Is

You'll find Georgialina in Georgia and South Carolina on both
sides of the Chattooga on down and across the Savannah River
into the South Carolina heartland and lowcountry all the way
to rice country. It lives there, and it lives in the heart.

In the South, perhaps more than any other region, we go back to our home in dreams and memories, hoping it remains what it was on a lazy, still summer's day twenty years ago.

Willie Morris, *North toward Home*

CONTENTS

Swinging to and fro beneath a stout oak limb kicked up
a breeze that made a sweltering day more tolerable.

A SENSE OF PLACE, A SENSE OF LOSS

Does a Southland live in your heart? Glancing at a map, do you recall childhood memories? When I see the Weather Channel's radar of the Southeast, there on the green county-outlined map I see the land of my youth, Lincoln County, Georgia. As a squall line sweeps across it, I recall the land of my fathers. Their clapboard homes, country stores, fire towers, outhouses, barns, windmills gave the land character.

Three hunters follow a brace of pointers through October broom straw as the sun drops through an orange-blue horizon. Those men were my kin, and I followed them afield.

A country store's candy bins overflow with Mary Janes and pink, white, and chocolate-striped coconut candy. Candied scents mingle with the woodsy scent of pine floors. My granddad owned that store. A gas pump sat out front. A minnow tank stood by the side.

Rain rinses dust from the kudzu covering the storm shelter where my family sought refuge from a tornado one night.

Rain pockmarks my aunt's pond where my grandmother taught me that a dragonfly landing on your cork brought good luck.

To this day the strangely beautiful whine of chainsaws and the clean, turpentined smell of felled pines comfort me. My dad cut pulpwood when I was a boy.

The fragrance of mown grass brings Friday night lights and the colliding sounds of shoulder pads and helmets to life.

I see more beauty in an emerald stand of bamboo than I do in a rose garden. It was my boyhood toy store, a storehouse of peashooters, flutes, and walking sticks. To this day it gives me a rush.

Childhood crackled with excitement. I heard stories about a plague that wiped out Petersburg, a town now beneath a lake. I rediscovered rapids long thought flooded where my mother's family picnicked when she was a child. Too many things she loved are gone. Much of what I loved doesn't exist. I like to write about childhood's joys. "Magic Was in the Air" conjured up childhood snows. William B. Keller knew how I felt.

> Your story brought to mind all those winters I prayed for snow when I grew up on Northeast Alabama's Sand Mountain plateau. One night in February 1958, anywhere from 8 to 14 inches of snow fell. My prayers were more than answered as I watched chicken-feather-size flakes blow across the yard, caught in the light from the front stoop. I'd run out into the front yard every 15 minutes to measure it with a ruler.

More weighty matters weren't so easily assessed. It was a time when the children of field hands and I played baseball in pastures where cow piles were bases. We knocked down red wasp nests and fished in ponds full of bluegill. When we went our separate ways come school we thought nothing of it. It was just the way things were.

When we were growing up, all seemed solid and secure. Wind would blow down a tree. A barn might burn, but nothing changed otherwise. The people I lived among never moved; they just died. I thought that uncomplicated land would last forever. How wrong I was. I went off to college, and a landscape new and strange heaved up. Ever since, I've struggled with the fleeting nature of people and places. What's more placeless than this homogeneous world with its strip malls, franchises, box stores, and fast-food chains, and it seems to be getting even more placeless.

I wrote a column bemoaning corporate-run cemeteries with their plastic flowers. In "A Place to Rest" I wrote of old cemeteries' grandeur. Jack deJarnette of Pensacola, Florida, thanked me:

> It was in this cemetery that seven young men met each morning for devotionals. A large oak tree had fallen just beyond some graves and was perfect for the seven of us to kneel as we prayed

together. The smell of decaying wood and leaves was rich and earthy. It was a place of peace, holiness, and wonder. I haven't thought of that place of my early faith formation in years. Thanks for taking me back. I actually, for a moment, caught the fragrance and wonder of those early morning meetings.

"Old Home Places" discusses the emotions you get when you see an old home place. Peggy Roney wrote me, "Going along a two-lane blacktop, old chimneys surrounded by weeds growing high and orphaned by their homes long gone, always leave me feeling homesick."

Homesick is a terrible illness. I left Georgia as a young man and long wanted to return to my homeland. One day a way back came about as a happy accident. My sister, Debra, bumped into my hometown paper's news editor, Jacquelyn Johnson. "Would your brother write a weekly column for us for free?"

"Why not," I told my sister. I began to write about the world I used to know. Thus began an examination of many things Southern. I wrote a lament, "Hunting's Long Demise—Do Boys Still Follow Men Afield?" Norman Hill wrote me:

> Hunting as we once knew it is pretty much a thing of the past. If you want to quail hunt, you make reservations at a "plantation" and shoot pen-raised birds conveniently planted throughout the property. Of course you get to ride on a genuine old-timey mule wagon for the "shonuff" Southern experience. All at a price. These days the shotguns don't come out of the safe too often, and God knows who will end up with them. My son used to enjoy hunting with me but has other interests these days. My grandson is a vegetarian. Probably not a lot of interest there in granddad's old shotguns. Today's kids know how to text and tweet and Facebook and chat on the cell phone for hours, but they don't know a sweetgum from a hickory.

Nor do many know what life was like for earlier generations. Some of us must preserve things. We can't let everything slip through our fingers. Writing this book kept me longing for the past, and from that longing rose a land of memories and experiences called *Georgialina: A Southland as We Knew It*. It's my hope it brings you a sense of place and soothes your sense of loss for things that are no more.

In olden days couples jouncing on joggling boards often found
themselves bouncing into jewelry stores for wedding rings.

PHOTOGRAPH BY THE AUTHOR.

FORGOTTEN BY TIME

My childhood church had open windows so breezes could cool fervent worshipers. Still, it was fashionable and practical to use hand-held fans. Open windows meant wasps, and those old fans shooed away many a flying menace. What fun it was to see a wasp land on a bald man's head during a boring sermon. Well, you can thank air-conditioning for doing away with that bit of entertainment.

Times were simpler way back when. People swept their yards with dogwood branches. Starry-eyed couples didn't date: they sat on joggling boards. And you could buy some white lightning from folks like my granddad. The moonshiner who made the South's high-spirited beverage was an outright folk hero. Revenuers be damned.

Prohibition and dry counties created fine careers for moonshiners, and white lightning assumed iconic status.

Now and then a backroad drive brings me across a tenant home. In their heyday these little shacks sat on rock piles surrounded by vegetable gardens where chickens pecked in the dirt. Some held an old pie safe and jars filled with cornmeal, flour, and grits. You could be sure a country store was close by. The tenant homes are collapsing and the country stores are closed. And who among you has eaten polk salad and stone-ground corn bread? Georgia and South

Carolina have ghost towns inundated by a lake, but when the water is down you can see evidence of these once-fine towns. The land has lost a lot of character. . . . As time moved on, people forgot the old ways and places, but they live on here.

A CHURCH FULL OF WASPS

Central air-conditioning took a lot of joy and beauty out of Sunday services. It meant closing the windows for good. Forget open windows with screens. Windows today are shut for good. Out went the ceiling fans and handheld fans, which funeral homes gave away as a form of advertising. We needed those elegant fans with the ice-cream-stick-like handles. Attending church should be a bit painful. In blazing summer heat you fanned away. The rhythms of those fans proved mesmerizing, and it gave a congregation an altogether pleasant animation.

Full-color reproductions of the Last Supper or Jesus on the cross fell prey to the greedy energy-devouring behemoths called central air-conditioners which necessitated sealed windows. Those closed windows did other damage too. They blockaded wasps, a great tonic for boring sermons. Nothing gets folks riled up like a mean old wasp flying around, and when a lot of wasps fill the air, the fun begins. I got much joy watching red wasps flit about the sanctuary at New Hope when I was a boy.

I knew from experience that a wasp sting ranks among the worst stings. It makes a bee sting seemed like a kiss. Imagine a heat-reddened needle jabbing you. Now that's a red wasp sting. And so it was with keen interest that I watched red wasps flutter about in New Hope Church in the 1960s. Throughout my boyhood, I was certain a wasp would nail a member of the congregation someday, giving me a memory for life.

All this wasp foolishness came about quite by accident. I was re-searching material for a book I was writing on the blues and how the shag developed when I came across a 1953 newspaper with a small news item buried low on the front page. There it was: "Wasp Disturbs Church Service."

I couldn't read the little story without smiling.

A buzzing wasp came near upsetting a church service Sunday at the Ocean Drive Presbyterian Church. The church's pastor, Rev. Howard C. Leming, in the midst of his sermon was "dive-bombed" by a big wasp which came down out of the church's rafters.

After discreetly dodging the insect's assaults for several minutes, the harassed minister cut loose and swatted at the pesky varmint with a hymnbook. Finally the wasp flew down into the congregation and lit on the top of a bald-headed church member who swatted him into eternity.

The subject of the pastor's sermon for the day was "Temperance and Temper and How to Control Them." Reverend Leming said later that he was "thankful for the opportunity of illustrating his sermon with a vivid example."

Well, there's something about bald heads that wasps like. Maybe a gleaming pate looks like an airfield to Mr. Wasp. Maybe it sends out a secret signal that says, "All clear for landing!"

How well I remember watching a wasp come in like a glider one day to make a perfect landing on Mr. Harvey Bonner's bald head. I was sitting right behind him with a bird's-eye view of the incident. Though he was fully focused on the sermon, Mr. Harvey knew something was up, literally. I saw a tiny flex of a neck muscle. And then he sat as still as a stone while that wasp cakewalked around his bald head. A deacon, he had no choice but to be stoic.

The wasp tap-danced on his head for five minutes. I half-expected its mesmerized mate to fly down and start building a nest. But no other wasps arrived. The bold wasp that had staked a claim to Mr. Harvey's head crawled around in tight circles, flexing its wings as if it were about to take off. It crawled north, south, east, and west. And then it raised its shiny blue tail, and I just knew Mr. Harvey was about to get a jolt from Hell itself. But no, it just wagged its tail up and down like it was practicing stinging.

"Shoot," I thought. "That wasp's a dud."

After sufficiently mapping Mr. Harvey's head, the venomous critter crawled down the side of his head, stepping onto the man's right ear. I was secretly praying, "Oh Lord, don't injure Mr. Harvey, but do let this wasp releaseth its stinger into yond man's ear."

After doing a few pirouettes on the tip of his ear, the wasp set sail and returned to the ceiling, where the cycle began anew.

Now most folks would lie and say, "Oh I'm sure glad that wasp didn't hurt that fellow." Not me. I wanted the wasp to sting Mr. Harvey good. Not do him harm, of course, but create a disturbance. I was curious as to what he might do when the wasp let him have it. Perhaps he would have silently endured the pain, or maybe he'd have shouted "Hallelujah! Praise be to God" and run outside. Or most likely he would have slapped the wasp into eternity like that fellow in Ocean Drive did in 1953.

I don't ever see wasps in church nowadays. One of the great steps backward in church entertainment was the advent of central air-conditioning. Sure makes fun in church hard to come by. All the windows are sealed shut. Central air does its job quietly and efficiently, and the wasps? Well, they are nowhere to be found.

Before New Hope installed central air, wasps were regular attendees at Sunday services. They'd cluster by the handful up in the ceiling where the electric lamp cords attached to the ceiling. As other wasps joined the fun, the cluster would get bigger and bigger. Then, suddenly, it was too big! That's when it fell toward the congregation, a swarming ball of evil.

As it fell, the wasps broke away one by one and flew back to the ceiling. A few wasps, however, no doubt disoriented, would buzz the congregation, causing great spurts of joy to fill my heart. Older ladies in hats would bat their funeral-home fans about with more zest than usual, and I can assure you their eyes were not on the preacher. Oh, no. They were following every move those satanic wasps made.

And then that one courageous wasp risked being swatted into eternity by landing on Mr. Bonner's head. Too bad it was such a dud. One of the great disappointments in my life will always be the fact that not once did a wasp sting a church member during Dr. Warren Cutts's soul-cleansing, sleep-inducing sermons.

And Mr. Harvey? He should receive a posthumous Purple Heart for the courage he displayed so many years ago.

THE JOGGLING BOARD

One summer day traveling a back road with friends I made a prediction. "When we hit the town up ahead I bet we'll see a trampoline for sale." Sure enough, as soon as we entered the town limits there it was, leaning against the wall of a Western Auto. My friends broke into laughter and accused me of having been through the town before.

Not true I said. It's just that more than a few times I've noticed how small-town stores always have a trampoline for sale. The people who sell trampolines must be pretty good. In many a small town, as soon as you hit the town limits, there it is: a trampoline leaning up against a store. Propping one up against a wall amounts to a billboard of sorts and it's hard to miss. "For sale." Get your jumps here.

Jump on oh trampoliners of the world, but understand that backyard bouncing is nothing new. I present the joggling board. I've often heard folks speak about joggling boards. Trying to envision that mind-joggling contrivance always made me stop and wonder. What exactly is it? I had a hazy notion of a resilient plank on supports, sagging in the middle and wide enough to accommodate a load of average derrières.

While sitting upon this pleasingly pliant board, you joggle. Now the *New Oxford American Dictionary* defines "joggling" as to "move or cause to move with repeated small bobs or jerks." As you joggle or bob up and down, an infinitesimal space comes between the plank and your backside. During that split second gravity pulls you and your fellow jogglers toward the center of the earth. Ever so gradually you slide toward one another. There was a great thrill to be had here. For young men and women out sparking, the joggling board was yesteryear's equivalent to parking.

The joggling board. It was an old-time backyard amusement that entertained folks of all ages in simpler times. Back then kids couldn't whip out their iPhone or Droid and send text messages to cross-town friends. They could joggle, though, but the joggling board required your friends to be with you. Imagine that.

Appropriately enough, I first saw a joggling board in the South Carolina lowcountry. It's a wide, flexible board that seems incapable of breaking no matter how many kids pile onto it. Of course, today's scale-smashing Tater Tot gobblers will give a joggling board a run for its money. Joggle, joggle, joggle, crack, pow . . . all come tumbling down in a pile of pine splinters.

The joggling board of yesteryear was a fixture in many backyards. As you'd expect, it has a colorful past, but, as you may not expect, it comes to us from Scotland by way of the South Carolina lowcountry. According to legend, the joggling board's origin stems from the pursuit of good health. It gave people a way to exercise. (You'd think that before electricity, power tools, and conveniences came along, people got plenty of exercise.)

The story goes that the first joggling board was built at Acton Plantation near Stateburg, South Carolina, the small town where Mary Boykin Chestnut, Civil War chronicler, was born. Cleland Kinloch built Acton Plantation in 1803, and when his wife died, his sister, Mrs. Benjamin Kinloch Huger, came to Acton to care for the household.

Rheumatism bedeviled Mrs. Huger, and she wrote her relatives in Scotland bemoaning her lack of exercise. She had the side of her carriage removed so that her chair could be placed in it and she could go for a ride. To her, riding along a bumpy lane in a carriage translated to exercise, though I'm positive the horse got the better workout.

In response to her letter, her Scottish kin sent a diagram of a joggling board, telling her she could sit on it and bounce gently. That, they said, would be a bit more exercise, and a grateful horse agreed. Using the design sent from Scotland, the plantation's carpenter built a joggling board from local timber, no doubt longleaf pine. That first board was straight-grained and free of knots and cracks.

From this first board, joggling boards spread quickly to the yards and piazzas of the lowcountry. Its popularity still runs strong. Today only swing sets and hammocks rival joggling boards as backyard amusements down lowcountry way.

So just how does this quivering contraption do its magic? Rockers support a long board at each end. Several people can sit on the board and joggle. As they bounce, they gravitate toward the sagging center of the board. Soon they are snug against each other, through no fault of their own. That closeness made a couple's hearts beat faster in prim and proper times, and the joggling board also became known as the courting bench.

Legend holds that no daughter went unmarried in any antebellum home that had a joggling board. Many a proposal, it's said, was made on a joggling board. After a proper amount of joggling, rings jangled, and in time some jiggling around produced a brand-new family member. All the result of a springy plank that literally brought couples together.

This entertaining outdoor furniture became an everyday sight in the nineteenth century. They stood on Southern porches, in yards, and in piazzas. At first glance they looked black. Tradition mandates that joggling boards be painted "Charleston green," a dark, dark green.

The story goes that "Charleston green" came about when Union troops sent the Holy City buckets of black paint to help the war-ravaged citizenry spruce up Charleston's appearance. A colorful lot, Charlestonians added green and yellow paint to the buckets (ten ounces black paint, four ounces green paint, and one-half ounce yellow paint) brightening the mournful black.

Today the joggling board is on the comeback trail. Several companies in South Carolina make joggling boards today. Prices run from the high $400s up to nearly $700. It sounds like a good way to soothe a baby . . . just joggle away until the baby is asleep. Children of all ages love joggling boards, even children in their eighties!

This venerable backyard amusement is such a tradition in the lowcountry that its name graces businesses that range from a gift shop in arrogantly shabby Pawley's Island to a publisher in Charleston, the Joggling Board Press. On its website the Press states that "the joggling board is an apt metaphor for the spirit of Joggling Board Press. . . . Joggling boards are long, capable of seating many at one time. By joggling simultaneously, eventually everyone winds up side by side. So it is for the talented people who make up Joggling Board Press."

Down in Charleston the Old Charleston Joggling Board Company makes these backyard-bobbing machines. The company's tagline urges folks to "put a joggle in your life." The company claims it's shipped joggling boards to all 50 states and abroad for more than 50 years. If the company has shipped some to Scotland, then I'd say the joggling board has come full circle.

The next time you're in Charleston, should you come across a joggling board, give it a try. Perhaps you'll find one in a park or, more likely, on the veranda of an old mansion on some guided tour. Put some joggle in your life. Sit down and bounce. When you do you'll be maintaining a Southern tradition that's endured wars, fires, and hurricanes and I'm sure a few termites here and there.

·{ WHEN PEOPLE }· { SWEPT YARDS }

A good many summers back, folks in Georgialina were begging for rain. The land was dry as a bone. South Carolina and Georgia were about ten inches short in annual rainfall. Many lawns died, and their parched roots lost their grip on the soil. When a thunderstorm did rumble in, deluges washed topsoil away. Roots crawled across the ground like serpents, and yards looked like the Mojave Desert— brown, dusty, and windblown.

Many people were happy to resod their lawns, for we live in a time when the greener and thicker your grass, the more prestige you garner as a homeowner. I resod my yard with St. Augustine and all that green grass resurrected a memory long gone—the days when yards were sand, not grass. Let's return to the late 1950s.

My Grandfather Walker never worried about watering his yard, cutting it, or fertilizing it. He didn't worry about insects or moles or about keeping his lawn mower in tip-top shape. His children swept the yard. My mom remembers sweeping it with a broom made from a dogwood. The yard stayed clean and neat and looked so smooth it resembled the hard-packed sand of a beach.

That's right. People use to sweep their yards, and they took immense pride in having a clean yard. Some say this tradition came from

West Africa, where people had good reason for sweeping the yard at daybreak: to keep an eye on snakes. A snake crawling through grass leaves little to no track. A serpentine track in the sand, however, betrays the presence of a snake. Swept yards served as a kind of snake radar.

During antebellum times slaves swept yards, which were for growing flowers, not grass. Back then folks didn't worry as to whether grass was centipede or Bermuda. All grasses were looked upon as weeds, and weeds were the enemy of a plant called cotton.

What was vital was keeping that yard clean as a whistle, and the broom of choice was a dogwood branch, what my mom and Aunt Sister called a "bresh broom." Why dogwood? It's tough and lasts a long time, probably a lot longer than many of today's cheaper plastic-component lawn mowers.

Of course things change, and change can take a while but it will come. Most Saturday mornings you'll hear a chorus of lawn mowers enjoying a breakfast of grass. Hearing the rhythmic sweep of dogwood branches? Well, the end for that began a long time ago. And with the demise of swept yards kids' games like marbles began to fade. Ever tried shooting marbles in grass?

Didn't think so. Well, you can thank Edwin Budding for that.

In 1830, Budding, an Englishman, was watching a roller-blade machine smoothing fabric in a textile factory when an idea struck him. Why not combine a scythe with a wheel? That was the beginning of lawn mowers, and when the gasoline-powered lawn mower arrived, it changed everything in a hurry. Suburban homeowners bought them en masse and the lawn wars were on.

Today, the competition to have the most beautiful lawn is an obsession. Now we do things like remove thatch, aerate the lawn, apply weed and feed, sharpen blades so they cut not tear, install irrigation systems, and wring our hands over the dearth of rainfall that seems to be our lot now and then.

The world of swept yards is long gone. Was a sandy yard better for the environment? Well, you had no need to water it, no fertilizer runoff, no mowers venting exhaust fumes, and for sure it made for quieter times. Not only were there no loud mowers; there were no whining weed eaters and leaf blowers. How blissful.

Still, the fragrance of freshly mown yards is sweet. It's a satisfying thing to mow the yard and for many a boy profitable. The first money I made came from cutting grass. Dad paid me a dime to cut the front yard. I can still see him handing me that dime. I used an old manual mower, so I earned it.

They say what goes around comes around. As I write this recollection, a gallon of regular gas is $3.85 and a barrel of oil has hit $145 for the first time. Maybe we'll have no choice but to return to sandy yards. Or we could just paint our yards green.

There's a company in South Carolina, Always Green Grass Painting, that will paint your dead grass green, a practice common in professional sports arenas. I'm just not ready to see dead grass painted bright green running up against a vinyl-sided house. That's just not the South I grew up in, all that fakery. I'll take a swept yard over a painted yard, and I'm sure my Grandfather Walker would have, too. More than once he told us there were two things he wouldn't allow near his home: a rat and a cat. I'm sure he would have included snakes, too, and his swept yard was a good line of defense against all things snake.

Nature reclaims what is hers. . . . Granddad's house burned in 1964, a sad seldom-mentioned saga, sorrowful in more ways than one. The house was never rebuilt. Long after it burned I went back to see the home place. No sand. No grass. Plant succession had resumed after humankind's brief interruption. Pines and oaks towered over the old front yard, and a broken glass and a rusty enamel pot lay in tangles of vines. Snakes for sure were about.

·{ WHITE }· LIGHTNING

My home county was dry when I was growing up. The only adult beverages I heard of were Pabst Blue Ribbon and moonshine. I don't recall any referendums to change things. There must have been a few though because I heard a man at Mr. Clifford's store say that every time an alcohol referendum came up, the preachers and bootleggers defeated it.

Few things are as storied in the South as moonshine and moonshiners. The moonshiner is a folk hero, and his elixir smells like a blend of vodka and it's as clear as glass. Touch a burning match to a teaspoon of it and a pale violet flame dances and whorls like the Aurora Borealis. Touch your lips to that crystal clear liquid and a sting lingers.

Hooch, white lightning, mountain dew, corn liquor, moonshine, rot gut, whatever you call it, this spirit has long been a part of the lore of the South. Its roots go back to the 1790's Whiskey Rebellion, a time when a federal tax was imposed on whiskey. Illegal distillers began to make their own liquor. Making and running white lightning has been a tradition ever since. My grandfather made shine and the locals said his was the finest around.

A while back a friend showed me his jar of moonshine. True to form, it was in a 505, self-sealing Mason jar.

Distilled beneath the light of the moon, hooch played an overhyped role in NASCAR's history. The oft-told story goes that moonshiners modified their cars to outrun federal agents so that they could deliver their cargo of contraband. Fear of arrest and imprisonment can make a man drive pretty fast, mountain curves or not, but the reality is that not that many racers started out as bootleggers.

Junior Johnson, one of the early stock car racers in the North Carolina mountains, did have a connection with moonshine. He's gone "legit," marketing legally produced grain alcohol moonshine. Junior Johnson's Midnight Moon is sold in liquor stores, packaged in a clay jug or Mason jar.

Moonshiners provided a product people wanted. For sure, impurities and irresponsible distilleries injured people. Hooch made in radiators and hooch tainted with chemicals did some damage. What was safe to drink and what was not became a matter of debate and myths.

Back in the day a common test to see if moonshine was safe to drink involved pouring white lightning into a spoon and setting it afire. Supposedly a blue flame meant it was safe to drink. A red flame meant lead was present. Thus the phrase, "lead burns red and makes you dead." Today we know moonshine can be deadly no matter what color flame burns.

As for the drink, well it's a simple concoction. The main ingredients are water, sugar, corn, and yeast. The equipment needed to distill this mash is simple, too. A copper pot, water-filled barrel, and copper tubing coil for a condenser constitute the elements of a still. Sometimes an oak barrel is used to age the liquor and give it color.

Over the years I've heard that anyone buying excessive amounts of sugar is probably a moonshiner but that seems farfetched. I've heard, too, that many a fortune has been made making and running white lightning. I rummaged around a bit and found that corn whiskey can bring $45 to $120 a gallon today.

The peak time for making shine runs from June to October for two reasons: it coincides with the peak of the corn harvest and it's a time the leaves have yet to fall, thereby providing cover for the illicit activity.

This old Southern heritage still goes on today in ways that will surprise you. Modern times find ways to take old ways and clothe them in a shiny new suit. The moonshiner's spirit of resourcefulness is alive and well. The December 2011/January 2012 issue of *Garden & Gun*, a fine magazine about things Southern, runs a story on moonshine in its department "Talk of the South." That story, "Heritage Hooch," describes how a modern-day (legit) moonshiner proves every bit as resourceful as old legendary moonshiners. And here's the surprising part—the moonshiner's a woman.

Troy Ball, a Vanderbilt graduate and mother of three sons, two with special needs, is a modern-day moonshiner. According to the article, she and her husband opened Troy & Sons Distillers in Asheville, North Carolina, where they produce "an uberclean white whiskey with hints of vanilla, cucumber, and melon." Their product is finding a market at the Grove Park Inn and the Inn at Biltmore and is distributed throughout North Carolina.

Modern moonshine, for sure, has its devotees as it's certainly had fans in the past, some famous. "Well, between Scotch and nothin', I suppose I'd take Scotch. It's the nearest thing to good moonshine I can find." William Faulkner said that.

It seems there's a festival to celebrate just about anything you can think of. In New Prospect, South Carolina, just off I-26 near Spartanburg and not too far from the North Carolina line, folks hold the annual Moonshiners Reunion. The festival celebrates the moonshine tradition, banjo picking, and bluegrass.

Well, why not celebrate the moonshining tradition? It provided a product people wanted and no doubt some needed. The moonshiner was often portrayed as a poor man simply trying to make a living. Some folks saw in the moonshiner a man "beating the system." When the Prohibition era came along, the moonshiner's image soared. The hypocrisy of Prohibition was obvious. Politicians continued to drink, further elevating the romantic image of moonshiners.

It was hard work and risky. The dreaded revenuers would make you pay if they caught you with the goods. Today you can lose your property and vehicles if caught making hooch, and yet unflinching souls still make it.

My Granddad Poland and his brother made it. Granddad was born in 1903. When Prohibition hit he was just an 17-year-old boy, but he later saw the money to be made. I was hauling hay with one of the black field hands when I was just a boy myself. "Yore granddad, Mr. Johnny," said a fellow, "made the finest shine in the lower half of the county."

Dad told me that revenuers raided Granddad's still one morning. They chased him through the woods, briars, and bushes until all his clothes got ripped off. And then they caught him. They escorted him to the home place where he stood before his wife naked as the proverbial jaybird.

"Thelma, I'm going to Augusta to do some business with these gentlemen. I'll be back."

And he did come back, soon! When the revenuers went to confiscate his still and shine they were gone. Brother, Carey, and farmhands had hauled it all out to the middle of the Savannah River on a barge where they sunk all that fine hooch.

So, how do you know a jar of moonshine today when you see it? According to Matthew Rowley, a bona fide moonshine expert, there's only one surefire way to know. "The single, universal, and defining characteristic of moonshine is that it is made outside of the law. If you can buy it in liquor stores, it's not moonshine." Troy Ball might disagree, but I'll leave that to her and Matthew to sort out. What's not debatable is that moonshine, that high-spirited Southern heritage, continues to make its presence felt across the Southland, and legal or not it carries on a fine Southern tradition.

.{ GENUINE CORN BREAD }.
AND GREENS

Down South people eat collards and cornbread on New Year's Day to lure extra money their way. Collards represent green folding money and golden corn bread represents coins, gold ones. It's symbolic, it's ritualistic, but we don't just eat corn bread and greens to start the year. We eat these foods several times a week and you'd think we're all millionaires.

I asked a lady from Beaufort who religiously prepares greens and corn bread each New Year's Day if she's seen any money from her ritual.

"Not yet," she said.

That these two foods don't conjure up money doesn't matter. What matters is how good they go together, especially with black-eyed peas and pork roast. People love corn bread and greens and eat 'em all the time. For certain we're rich when it comes to Southern cooking. Things have changed though.

For most people the days of growing your own greens and buy-ing stone-ground meal are passé. These days, people buy big green clumps of collards held tight by rubber bands and boxed corn meal from the grocer. Jiffy Corn Muffin Mix comes to mind. Despite the convenience of packaged corn meal, a few gristmills eke out an exis-tence, and Mom told me where I could find one. I left her home in the Peach State one fine spring afternoon to head to Carolina. My destination was a rural outpost, a gristmill she and Dad had been to years ago. Since Dad passed she hadn't been back. I'd make the trip for her.

It was a good day to travel. Molten sunlight rained down, cot-tony clouds salted the deep blue sky, and newly minted leaves were as green as they'd be all year. It was a glorious day for a preordained mission: taking back roads to Price's Mill, for there was no other way to get there.

In McCormick I took Highway 28 toward Plum Branch, where I turned left onto Highway 283, a road that suggests the South of the 1950s. I had never been down this backroad, and traveling it was like time traveling. Knowing no interstate would wreck my day filled me with bursts of joy.

Signs directed me to older and narrower roads. Soon I was on a graveled-tar road of the old days where a roller-coaster plunge to Stevens Creek shot me right past the mill. Looking for a place to turn around, I spotted two men studying plants along the shoulder of the road. I shot past them, too. At the top of a hill gourds hung from a pole. When you see purple martin gourds you better believe you're in deep country.

Doubling back, I pulled over where the men were gathering long green stalks. I rolled down my window, and the younger fellow came up carrying a large, leafy plant.

"You getting up a mess of polk salad?" I asked.

"Yes suh. My mama says it's great. Gonna eat some tonight."

I had heard of polk salad (or "poke salad," as some folks call it) all my life. I had never eaten any, but I'd been told more than once that it tastes like spinach. Good for these hunter-gatherers, I thought, harvesting a free meal courtesy of a sun-dappled side road. Tony Joe White's "Polk Salad Annie" came to mind, a song that recounts the story of a poor Southern girl and her hungry family eating a wild plant that looks a bit like turnip greens.

The song doesn't tell us all we need to know about polk salad. It's poisonous. Country folk say it has to be "properly prepared," and that calls for boiling the plant in three changes of water. I'm sure the friendly fellow's mama knew just how to cook it. How fitting I thought were her name Annie.

Eager to see the old mill, I put the car in gear. "Hey," I shouted, "is the mill open today?"

"Shoot, dat thing's been shut down ten years."

"Damn," I thought. "Closed."

I coasted downhill over Stevens Creek and pulled onto a grassy slope that ran down to the mill. No paths led to the steps, and overgrowths of grass and bushes surrounded the mill and a Chevy pickup sat under its shed. Millstones sat idle on its stoop.

Inside the 1890 rough-hewn pine building R. A. Price ground some 14,000 pounds of cornmeal over a seven-day week. After he died, in 1968, his son, John M. Price, took over the crushing and pulverizing of yellow cornmeal.

When Price's Mill made the National Register of Historic Places, on November 22, 1972, it was one of South Carolina's few remaining water-powered gristmills. It saddened me to see the old mill out of business. Someday the millstones would fall through the porch and all would soon crumble.

In front of the mill stood a tractor overtaken by vines and saplings. A shrub covered the driver's seat. A tractor overturned and killed John Price, bringing an end to the old mill's run. That tractor in the vines? Surely it wasn't the one?

I resumed my journey thinking of how an overturned tractor had wrought an era's end. There'd be no authentic corn bread to go with these modern-day hunter-gatherer's greens tonight. I like to think that there was, though, that somehow they knew where to get stone-ground cornmeal. That somewhere on a picturesque stream an old mill ground away, creaking and laboring, pouring out gold cornmeal. That thought pleased me as I made my way back to the city.

As I approached Lexington, modern life asserted itself with vengeance. Traffic picked up, and I passed mobile homes, cell towers, high-voltage power lines, and a glossy medical facility. Billboards, quick stops, and orange traffic cones banished beauty. I had crossed the invisible line that decrees that old ways surrender to new. My car had forsaken the past where people found dinner along roadsides and men used falling water to grind cornmeal for I had crossed the border into a place called Urbanization.

The air left me.

I vowed to go back to Highway 283. There's beauty, majesty, and unparalleled richness along highways assigned to the 200s and I aim to travel more of them. In addition to polk salad, old ways still live along these forgotten highways where yesteryear makes its last stand.

·❧ GHOST TOWNS ❧·

Growing up, I watched old cowboy movies about ghost towns out West and even went to Ghost Town in the Sky in Maggie Valley, North Carolina. Little did I know I lived in an area with ghost towns nearby and what politics and history once lived there.

Three vanquished towns sprang up here long, long ago. And then the fates conspired to do them in. Petersburg was in Wilkes County, Georgia (later Elbert). Lisbon was in Lincoln County, and Vienna was near Mt. Carmel, South Carolina. Look at an old map and you'll see these towns weren't far apart. The *New Georgia Encyclopedia* says residents of Lisbon, Petersburg, and Vienna could all see one another's town. The Broad River separated Petersburg from Lisbon. The Savannah River set Vienna apart.

Suppose these three towns had grown over many decades into one "rivertropolis." Imagine a Georgia-South Carolina version of Venice, Italy, a place where waterways connect two states' shining city. It's tempting to speculate what the region might be like today had fate left a few things alone. Would the lake have been allowed to swallow prosperous places that expanded into one city more than 170 years or so?

We just can't know. All we know is that Petersburg got all the attention as the three vanquished villages go. Petersburg sprang up in the forks of the Savannah and Broad Rivers. For ten years, it ranked as Georgia's third-largest city behind Savannah and Augusta. Petersburg rose to prominence as a tobacco inspection site and had a post office and a newspaper. Entertainment in the form of plays, balls, promenades, picnics, and community celebrations made life interesting. Doctors, lawyers, and politicians lived there. Petersburg alone can claim a slice of political history: it clings to the distinguished honor of being the only town in the nation's history to produce two U.S. senators, William Bibb and Charles Tait, who served at the same time.

Petersburg and the Broad River valley served as a breeding ground for political alignments in Georgia during the early national period, especially between factions claiming Virginian ancestry and others connected with North Carolina families.

A series of bad things happened to this place of powerful politics. Cotton replaced tobacco as a cash crop, the steamboat's arrival robbed Petersburg of commerce beyond the fall line, and the Savannah and Broad Rivers prevented railroads from reaching it. New land to the west lured people away and Western Fever caused many remaining residents to abandon the area.

Until all this misery arrived, two sister towns had helped Petersburg grow. Tiny Lisbon, founded by Virginian Zachariah Lamar in 1786, sat just across the Broad River in Lincoln County. Vienna was founded around 1795 across the Savannah in South Carolina. Neither town achieved Petersburg's success.

A ferry connected all three and commerce flowed among them. As long as tobacco remained an important staple crop in the Broad River valley, Petersburg flourished. After being inspected in Lisbon or Petersburg, tobacco boats (they were called Petersburg boats) made their way to Augusta and back, a trip that took about a week.

Lisbon was a spot. Just a spot. Vienna surpassed Lisbon in everything, wrote the president of Emory College, the verbose Augustus Baldwin Longstreet, pointing out that "Lisbon we believe could never boast of more than two stores and a groggery, and as many dwellings. Vienna surpassed Lisbon in everything, but exactly how far, and in what we are not able to say, except in John Glover's house and store, which had no match in Lisbon."

Vienna was a lumber town, but research uncovers the fact that it also had an exclusive academy founded by Dr. Moses Waddell. At one time he was South Carolina's foremost educator, and he would become the fifth president of the University of Georgia. Without doubt the vicinity of Petersburg, Lisbon, and Vienna held enough intellectuals, leaders, and people of distinction to survive most anything and yet they didn't.

In time a massive wall of concrete and steel would rise, and Clarks Hill Lake would give all three a watery grave. The very water that birthed and separated them and connected them would bring the final insult but not without moments of fame.

Vienna made the *New York Times* way back in 1851. The subject was dueling, that chivalrous if deadly custom gentlemen used to settle their differences long ago. Dueling was long legal in South Carolina, but apparently it wasn't legal in Georgia. That's the conclusion I draw from the October 1, 1851, article in the *New York Times:* "Duel at Vienna, South Carolina." The article carries a Charleston, Tuesday, September 30, dateline. The story reads: "A duel was fought on Saturday between Mr. Smyth, an associate editor of the *Augusta Constitutionalist*, and Dr. Thomas, of Augusta, at Vienna, S.C. The cause of the duel was an article signed, 'Doctor,' in the *Chronicle* and *Sentinel*, offensive to Smyth, of which Thomas avowed himself to be the author. Upon the third fire the ball passed through Smyth's right thigh, and nearly through the left, but the wound is not considered mortal. He reached Augusta on Sunday night and is doing well. Thomas was not touched."

Well, okay, two Georgia boys crossed the Savannah to duel. No one died, and I suppose Smyth regained his honor. I suppose, too, that people talked excitedly of this settling of accounts as they traveled the ferry from Vienna to Lisbon to Petersburg. Dueling would not be part of Vienna's future because it didn't have a future. Nor did Petersburg or Lisbon. As Petersburg declined, its post office moved to Lisbon in 1844 and closed in 1855. Vienna disappeared.

One summer several years back when the lake was way down, I went to Petersburg by boat. I saw streets, sidewalks, and foundations where homes once stood, where businesses once thrived. But now they were relics of another time. I saw much flotsam, evidence of man's presence. I came away with a near-perfect milk glass disk. Held in the light just so, you can read "Genuine Boyd Cap For Mason Jars." Some long-ago dutiful woman perhaps used it to store tomatoes. Whatever it preserved, it wasn't Petersburg.

Petersburg I'd like to think could have and should have survived. Not only did it have river transportation but it was also part of the stagecoach route that ran south to Augusta. Another line ran from Milledgeville, Georgia, all the way to Washington, D.C. The future sure looked bright. And then a rapid decline and outright collapse ended everything.

I'll leave it to history to decide whether the lake was and is a good thing for the county, but we sure lost a lot of history when that lake covered the land. Big things like towns and natural gems like an old oak tree my Mom remembers up near Lisbon. "It was so big," she said, "five men could not link hands and reach around it."

Ferries, ancient towns, and massive oaks: they're all gone now. Spots across the Savannah where Georgians paced, turned, and fired to settle their differences? They're gone, too. And still I wonder. What might Lincoln County, Lincolnton, and even the Central Savannah River Area be like today had the three settlements prospered? What if these places with memorable European names—Petersburg, Lisbon, and Vienna—had not just survived but forged a regional focal point? Would that achievement been enough to discourage politicians from building a lake they could plaster their name on? Probably not.

As we became more urbanized and agribusiness arrived, family farms gave way, and people lost touch with what it takes to grow crops and livestock.

PHOTOGRAPH BY THE AUTHOR.

❧ OLD WAYS ❧

In the 1950s the fields and ponds on my granddad's farm were my hunting and fishing estate. Cane poles, worms, Zebco rod and reels, Little Cleos, and a Mossberg .410 shotgun were my companions. Every day was an adventure.

It was a time for outdoor exploits. Uncle Carroll told me how men would "call up" fish by the boatload. Talk to a kid today about telephoning fish, and he'll figure it's an Angry Bird–like app on a smartphone. What a colorful pastime telephoning was back in the day, and what great fish frys it supplied.

More and more children are growing up without contact with family farms, feed and seed stores, and the outdoors. How many kids today have plucked just-laid eggs from beneath a hen? More kids ride merry-go-rounds than mules and horses. Some men and women, however, still ride horses in pursuit of deer and bear. Boys just don't follow men afield like they used to. As the old hunters die out, their sons do not take up arms.

We're in retreat on all fronts. An old tradition of closing shop Wednesdays at noon is disappearing. That stolen piece of Saturday made for a good time to go fishing. And I'll guarantee you no one gets a wart removed today by an old-timer using broomstraw and an incantation. No more do people sit up all night with the dead.

Anyone heard cowbells echoing across a pasture at dusk of late? Things that made my boyhood beautiful and mysterious disappear bit by bit. It's nigh sunset, and the bugle sounds its ringing notes.

·{ DO BOYS STILL FOLLOW MEN AFIELD? }·

It's a classic late-afternoon, autumn day. Men in canvas jackets follow a pair of pointers working a brushy field. Sunlight slants low across the men. Guns reflect the light. The dogs edge forward, then freeze. The covey explodes and shots ring out as brass and red shells flash in the gloaming. The dogs fetch two quail and the men compliment them on their fine work.

Fall's arrival got my blood racing as a boy. A bite in the air and red and yellow leaves edged with frost meant hunting season had arrived. I dreamed of bobwhite quail and whitetail bucks, but it was just a dream. I was better at reading about hunting than at hunting itself. A magazine felt more comfortable in my hands than a gun did.

Outdoor Life brought adventure into my life. When I did go afield, deer, doves, and quail had nothing to fear. I was no tour de force when it came to hunting, but I tried for a while. I wanted to know the joy of bagging a bird on the wing.

"When you have shot one bird flying, you have shot all birds flying. They are all different and they fly in different ways but the sensation is the same and the last one is as good as the first." Hemingway wrote that, and I was eager to experience the sensation.

My parents gave me a Mossberg bolt-action .410 shotgun one Christmas. I loved oiling that gun and smelling the cordite when I shot it. I loved the stock; the fine-grained wood glistened. And the blue barrel was as solid as the Rock of Gibraltar. The slim shells felt perfect in my hand.

I dreamed about shooting birds, but I was no good. To become good at something you must do it over and over with success. No one taught me to shoot on the wing, and I often made a joke of my ineptness. "I couldn't shoot a quail if it flew down my barrel."

We tend to stop doing those things we're no good at. Any interest I had in guns and hunting faded, but life had a surprise waiting for me. I found myself working for a hunting and fishing agency. My boss made me hunt. "If you are going to write about hunting you need to do it," he said. On a Southern plantation dripping with Spanish moss, I shot my first and only deer. I never took up a gun again.

People began to disparage hunting. Erudite people classified people's love for outdoor recreation into categories. You could be a consumptive user or you could be a nonconsumptive user, which meant you hiked, watched birds, and camped among other activities that did not involve killing and eating, that is, consumption. All this divisiveness was unknown to me when I was a boy walking through woods with my .410 across my shoulder. Deep inside I loved hunting, and I still regret that I was no good at it.

A love for hunting, by and large, is something fathers pass on to their sons and daughters. Somewhere along the trail, too many fathers quit taking their sons and daughters afield. Too many guns stayed in the case.

Do little boys still follow men into fields and forests? Well, I didn't. Dad and I didn't hunt much together. We hunted rabbits just once. We never hunted deer. We had no rifles other than the Japanese infantryman's rifle Dad brought back from Hiroshima. We hunted turkey some and he took me quail hunting a time or two, but there seemed to be a big drop-off in hunting from my granddad's time to Dad's time. Why?

Maybe World War II sickened a generation of men of guns. Maybe it became too much bother and expense to hunt when starting a family and paying bills. Boys don't follow men into fields and forests anymore. Their dads are not around like before, and besides more and more boys live in the city.

The hunter is now an endangered species. So what, you say. Well, this is what. Drive with alertness. Your chance of hitting a deer will rise. Get ready for new taxes. Monies hunters spend earmarked for conservation will fall. Expect bad behavior. More boys may become delinquents as this responsible father-son ritual dies out.

In a culture that's increasingly antihunting, I am not an antihunter. I've written about hunting, but I don't hunt. I can't recall the last time I ate venison. Hunting has its place in the modern world. It's part of our heritage, it helps keep game populations in check, and it provides great outdoor recreation for sportsmen. It does much to fund the preservation of woods and fields as well. But the times they are a-changing. As the old saying goes, "Your hunter today is not your grandfather's hunter."

So, who is your typical hunter today? He's a 42-year-old white guy. He lives in a land where suburbs consume forests and fields and a lot of people disapprove of his hobby. Animal rights activists have their crosshairs on him. Moreover, becoming a gun owner grows more and more difficult, as is finding a place to hunt.

And so hunting's long, slow demise continues. It lives here and there on plantations and is more of a business than a tradition. And so the South loses more of its charm and character as Norman Rockwell–like hunters afield fade to black.

Deep in my treasure chest of memories is a golden fall afternoon in the late 1950s. I want to say it is 1959. It's late afternoon, a cold day. In the west, a tincture of gold light overdrips a blood-red horizon. Ahead of me walk Granddad Poland and Uncle Joe. Their breath hangs in the air like smoke. A shotgun rests comfortably over each man's shoulder. They have been hunting quail on the farm. Two dogs lead the way back to the farmhouse, where a fragrant plume of wood-smoke smudges the sky.

I tagged along to share secondhand that fine sensation Hemingway described. That was more than a half-century ago. For the life of me I cannot recall if they found birds, and that tells me a lot. Hunting is not so much about the kill as it is the experience, and that experience seems old-fashioned to people well fed on slaughterhouse meat. And it is not appealing to boys who shoot digital guns at Earth-invading monsters, nor is it appealing to city boys who'd rather shoot pool.

Yes, the old hunters are dying out. Their sons do not take up arms. And hunting's long, slow demise continues. God forbid we lose our modern contraptions and the electricity they depend on. If that day arrives, a lot of people will have to learn to hunt. I'm not sure they can, but hunger is one hell of a motivator.

⟨ TELEPHONING FISH ⟩

Let me say up front that this is not about a fellow who placed a call to Charlie the Tuna. No, it's a trip down memory lane thanks to an old-timer. We were talking about bream beds, white bass running, and swapping fishing tales when he got a gleam in his eye. "Son," he said, "if you can find an old crank telephone you can catch all the catfish you want."

It sounded too good to be true. He then told me about some men back in the 1950s who would "call up fish" at shoals and other rocky waters. "Caught gunny sacks full," he said. I daresay few folks are around who've cranked an old-time telephone, but if any of you have you are a bona fide old-timer.

The fishing bonanza new lakes created in the late 1940s and early 1950s led to this legendary, if unethical, way to catch catfish. You didn't need a rod and lures or a cane pole and red wigglers. You just needed an old telephone and a scoop net. You never got a busy signal but boy you'd be busy scooping up fish.

Telephoning proved especially popular down South in the early 1950s, perhaps one of this country's greater decades. Great that is unless you were a catfish swimming along doing what catfish do best, scavenging. Here you are down on the bottom easing along looking for a meal when all of a sudden a jolt hits you. Next thing you know, the world is a bright, waterless place. Soon, your new neighbors are hush puppies and coleslaw and you owe your demise to an old telephone but not just any phone.

Conjure up an image of Sheriff Andy Taylor cranking an old phone to get Mayberry's operator, Sarah. That's the kind of phone we're talking about. As Sheriff Taylor cranks the handle, a magneto fires out as much as several amps and 110 volts.

Western Electric made a lot of those classic old phones, phones destined to find another life of sorts in a boat. When rotary-dial telephones began to replace the old crank phones, the scrap heap didn't get all those vintage phones. Enterprising folks found new uses for the old telephones' magnetos, a five-dollar word for generator. Somebody discovered that cranking the old telephone while dangling its positive and negative wires out of a boat would bring fish up by the dozens. It was a shocking discovery to say the least . . . especially if you were a catfish without scales. Fish species with scales seem immune to this fishing fad from the 1950s.

Telephoning worked especially well in shoals where rocky bottoms made for a stronger electrical current, hence more stunned catfish. The current doesn't kill them. It just stuns them long enough for a fellow with a scoop net to grab them when they float up. And soon all that fish frying begins.

Telephoning became so widespread that catfish populations began to plummet, and then the surviving catfish wised up. Some observers of all things catfish believed the smarter catfish would vamoose when they heard a boat motor approaching or heard wires scraping across the rocky bottom. This belief stemmed from the fact that fewer fish floated to the surface. Well, here's a thought: most likely they had been fished out, telephoned to death. It got so prevalent that folks began to outlaw it. In 1955 in if you got caught calling up catfish you'd land on the chain gang for 30 days.

I'd heard my parents talk about this easy way of fishing. They heard about people who called up catfish. Mickey Cliatt, an old classmate back in Georgia, called me up one day to talk about telephoning. He told me some men in the Double Branches of Lincoln County, Georgia, long ago would regularly telephone fish and hold a big fish fry open to the community. People came from miles to enjoy the food and fun.

More than a few communities would dispatch men with a crank phone to some rocky-bottomed river. The goal was to "catch" a couple hundred pounds of catfish. The whole community would come and bring covered dishes and what have you, like a Sunday picnic on church grounds or a potluck supper. A big fish fry back in simpler times was a big-time event, and it kept people close even if the fishing was unethical.

Human nature tends to favor the easy way out, and the easy way out all too often leads to abuse and the legislation of laws. It was just a matter of time before telephoning became illegal. Of course that didn't stop some folks. Nothing like some easy, illegal hunting and fishing to bring out the competitive spirit. That anything-you-can-do-I-can-do-better attitude. Back in 1954 two fishermen over Oklahoma way came up with the most devastating system yet for shocking catfish to the surface. They attached wires to their outboard motor's magneto. When they started up the motor, catfish surfaced all over the water wherever they went.

The shock was strong; the shock was steady. In fact, it was so potent that the overjoyed "fishermen" were promptly knocked into the water when they reached overboard to gather their bountiful harvest. They were as paralyzed as the catfish they tried to scoop up and would have drowned except for a game warden's timely arrival. He shut off their motor and pulled them out. When they came to, he arrested them.

It's too bad plentiful resources get abused. The people who settled this country were astounded at the vast numbers of waterfowl and fish here. Like Mike Tyson and all his boxing millions, they thought such good fortune would last forever. Wrong.

People squandered natural resources left and right. We have departments of natural resources today thanks in part to things like punt guns and telephoning. People just can't resist the easy way out.

Nothing new here. Those most respected sportsmen, the Native Americans, made hooks from bone and shells and fishing lines from vines. That didn't stop them, however, from using green walnut husks to drug fish. The husks would leach toxins into the water, and, as in telephoning, stunned fish would float to the surface for easy picking. I don't advise any of you would-be catfish callers to try either of these methods.

Today many states have laws on the books whose language goes something like this: "The introduction of electrical currents or physical shocks for the purpose of taking fish is prohibited." If you drop a line into the water, it better not be an old telephone line. Get caught doing that and you will be the one who gets a shock, a 30-day-in-jail, $300-fine type of shock.

HUNTING ON
HORSEBACK

It's a cold, blustery December morning. Three horsemen lean into a biting wind at Oaklawn Plantation. With hollowed horns strapped across their backs, they ride through fire-blackened longleaf pine, their marsh tackies near invisible in the thick underbrush and tall grass. Their quest? Heritage and deer. Trailing a pack of dogs, the trio drops out of view of the standers placed strategically along the edges of woods, only to emerge downrange. As they quietly weave in and out of thick underbrush, their movements take on an almost dreamlike quality.

A whitetail breaks from cover. Whoops, hollers, and cracking whips shatter the morning's calm. A cinematic blur of movement swirls through the trees. The horsemen rally the dogs to drive the deer toward standers, and a salvo of shots reaps a deer.

A second drive gains three more deer, but a wounded buck runs hard toward a flooded cornfield with the dogs in close pursuit. Two blows on the horn light a fire under the horsemen. Brothers Ed and Rawlins Lowndes and David Grant ride after the hounds.

Rawlins Lowndes, commanding the hounds, rides Grant's marsh tacky, Sage, and Grant rides DP. Ed Lowndes rides Laboka, captured from a wild herd on Hilton Head Island. They have the right horses for the task at hand. Saplings, low-hanging limbs, tangled vines, armadillo holes, bushhog amputees—small-tree stubble—and thick, tall grass make the going rough for any horse. The marsh tacky, though, is not any horse.

The deer plunges into the flooded field with hounds in hot pursuit, and Rawlins Lowndes, carrying a shotgun borrowed from a stander, pounds around the edge of the dike surrounding the field, zigzagging between small trees and dodging low-hanging limbs. He urges Sage up the embankment, and up he goes through thick grass studded with perilous holes.

Lowndes and Sage reach the far bank just ahead of the deer. Is a clean shot possible? On top, the dike is a narrow sliver, and it's a long way down to the bone-chilling water. Lowndes weighs his options as the deer turns back, narrowly flanking the dogs. By this time, Grant and DP have caught up, and Rawlins hands the shotgun to Grant, who gallops off, trying once again to cut off the deer's escape route. As the deer catapults up the dike, Grant closes in. BAM!

DP doesn't even flinch.

Lowcountry hunting on horseback resonates with tradition, and that agile breed the Carolina marsh tacky boasts an enduring legacy. "Tacky" comes from an English word meaning "common" or "cheap." Hogwash. A small band of men (and women), among them David Grant and Ed and Rawlins Lowndes, knows the horse is worth a king's ransom. They hunt deer and wild hogs as men before them did—from horseback—and they intend to keep hunting atop the marsh tacky a South Carolina tradition.

The Lowndes family has hunted on horseback for five generations. Grant owns and operates Carolina Marsh Tacky Outfitters and breeds tackies. He brought three of his horses to the hunt at Oaklawn. The American Livestock Breeds Conservancy estimates that fewer than 150 pure marsh tackies exist, though breeders and advocates for the horse are trying to change that.

Somewhere an anthem plays for the marsh tacky, Procul Harum's "Conquistador." As early as the 1500s, Spanish ships anchored along South Carolina's coast. Their cargo included measles, smallpox, and chicken pox, but it also included fine-boned horses, a measure of absolution. The Spaniard's colonies failed, and the would-be colonists left their horses to fend for themselves near Myrtle Beach and Port Royal. "Conquistador your stallion stands in need of company" goes the song. Company it found.

In the 1600s, stunned English explorers beheld Cherokee and Chickasaw Indians riding small, rugged horses. The Gullah tilled their fields and gardens using tacky power. During World War II, beach patrols seeking Nazi U-boats rode marsh tackies. Had spies slipped ashore, men on marsh tackies would have been the first line of defense. No surprise there. The horse had already ridden into the history books. It's believed the legendary Swamp Fox, Francis Marion, led his irregulars into guerrilla-like forays on the sturdy yet nimble horses. Marsh tackies would have easily outflanked the British Army's larger European breeds in the woods and swamps. Today the horses pursue a quarry that's a bit of a guerrilla fighter itself—wild Pee Dee hogs.

It's a Saturday in August, and today's band of equestrians and hunters includes the Lowndes brothers, Grant, Richard Perdue, Bryan Stanton, Moultrie Helms, and their guide, Troy Byrd. Other participants include tacky devotee Wylie Bell, a writer/designer, and photographer Dwain Snyder.

A day that began in heavy fog has turned hot enough to melt pig iron in Roblyn's Neck, a 14,000-acre tract along the Great Pee Dee River. By now, wild hogs with any sense have retired to the most unpleasant pieces of real estate possible, thick scrub and briar thickets. The sun pours down, and, thundering down a lane scraped from ancient sea bottom, the horses kick up contrails that hang in the air. Time suspends as well—it looks like a scene from the wild, wild West.

According to Grant, marsh tackies "take the gunfire, briars, and blood better than most. I will ride a cutdown with the wind coming to me and pick my way from spot to spot where I think a deer will be bedded. When he rips up, you better be quick and you better have a good horse."

But today is about hogs, and as the day heat ups, so does the action. The land echoes with the yelps, yowls, and yaps of Pee Dee curs, a dog Grant describes as the "noble Pee Dee game dog."

"When you hunt hogs," says Grant, "you need dogs that can think, 'Plenty of signs, but no hogs. Where are they?' You need a dog that can work an area and find a hog bedded down in a blowdown or more often in the middle of a hellhole cutdown. It's tough!"

The music dog hunters love sounds out—a howling bay that signals the dogs have cornered their quarry. That epic do-or-die last stand unfolds. A banshee-like squeal makes the hair stand on your neck. Riding point, Grant and company gallop off, puffs of dust bursting from unshod hooves. "Most of the time," said Grant, "I ride point. I get the honor of being the first to bust up briars, jump a ditch, cross or swim a slough, or dodge snakes." A good point horse, he adds, "will go to the bay on its own when it hears the dogs."

Closer to the dogs, bedlam—pig squeals and chaotic dog vocals. Grant plunges through head-high brambles, briars, and undergrowth, clawing his way to the action. There's Bill, diminutive leader of the curs, nipping at a 200-pound sow.

Grant hunts with a GPS tracking system that gets him to the bay quicker than in the old days. "I often ride right into a fight if my dogs are getting cut up from a bad hog." Grant has a pact with his dogs. "If they have the grit to hunt all day, fight everything a Pee Dee river bottom can throw at them, run a hog through Hell and back, and fight to the death if need be, I will do whatever it takes to get to them." For that task, the marsh tacky has no equal.

Wylie Bell first learned about the marsh tacky when she interviewed Grant about the Hilton Head Marsh Tacky Beach Run. She ended up riding one of Grant's tackies at Hilton Head. "The first thing I noticed," she said, "was how easily tackies adapt to new situations. Here were these five-year-old horses thrown into a thousand people, racing horses next to a rolling ocean. And they handled it amazingly well. People were crowding around them all day, and no one got kicked or bitten or run over by a spooked horse."

Later, Bell discovered the marsh tacky's hardy character. "My first hog hunt opened my eyes to how tough the breed is. I'm always careful to watch for fallen limbs, holes, uneven terrain, muddy spots—anything that could cause a horse to trip. On a hog hunt, you run full speed through mud and muck and cutdowns with stumps, holes, logs, and briars. The horses never miss a beat. They don't panic when they get wrapped up in briars or when they're mired in a bog up to their chest. Like little bulldozers, they push through whatever you ask them to."

Pursuing deer in December and wild hogs in August, tilling gardens, racing at Hilton Head, defeating the British, patrolling for German subs, and anchoring a tradition, the marsh tacky does it all. What else can be said about this horse for all seasons? Bell hits the nail on the head.

"The marsh tacky is simply better put together to handle riding in the woods and swamps. They're smaller and more agile, their hide is thicker, and they have good, solid hooves. Marsh tackies are not big horses, but they ride big. They have huge hearts and sharp minds, and for people who own them, they'll be that horse of a lifetime."

·{ FAMILY FARMS }·
MELT AWAY

I read that 25 things are about to disappear in the United States. Some you will be glad to see go, and some, well, I wonder how we'll adjust once they pass into history.

Here's what's on the way out: the Post Office, yellow pages, classified ads, movie rental stores, telephone land lines, swimming holes, answering machines, incandescent bulbs, handwritten letters, personal checks, and TV news programs. Topping the list is something that causes me to shake my head. The family farm.

When I was a boy I spent many summer days at my granddad's farm. It was a rolling land of several thousand acres with ten or more ponds. White-faced cattle roamed the pastures. Pink, white, and mint-green salt blocks stood out against the grass. Besides cattle, Granddad grew watermelons and cotton, and he and the field hands grew gardens filled with tomatoes, okra, corn, and at times collards. I could walk out of the farmhouse where a back room held mounds of zigzagged striped watermelons through a fence to a henhouse and from there to a barn deep with years of manure on to two fishponds teeming with fish. I never hurt for anything to do.

When Granddad died of a heart attack the summer of 1972, my dad and my aunt inherited their shares of the farm. In time Dad sold his. My aunt continued to raise cattle until she retired. Today Granddad's farm sits idle. For all practical purposes it is gone. Another statistic and another sad story repeating itself across the South.

The U.S. Department of Agriculture says we had 5.3 million farms in 1950. Today we have a shade over 2 million. According to Farm Aid, 330 farmers leave their land every week. As family farms shut down, most are not replaced. Very few young people become farmers today. The old guard of lifelong, reliable farmers is about to leave us. Then what?

To understand the South you had to understand farming—the backbone of life for many. Just about everyone had a garden, and a lot of folks canned their own vegetables. Families got their hands in dirt. Folks grew much of what they needed and so a fixture of those days was the indispensable feed and seed store, the farmer's best friend. Entering such stores was a sensory experience filled with fertile smells and colorful sacks. It's been a while since I poked around in a venerable feed and seed store (yet another experience today's younger set will miss).

I wrote about an old feed and seed store that Columbia's urban sprawl was swallowing whole. It had boot-worn wooden floors, pine heart columns, and a patina of peeling green and white paint. There was a time you could leave the old store and all you'd see were fields, gardens, tangled undergrowth, and fallow land.

The old store was there, though, there for a long time. Walking into it meant entering air heavy with a medley of scents . . . the peppery aroma of cured leather, the pungent smell of insecticide, sweet bouquets of livestock feed, the dry but fertile whiff of cracked corn, mellow smells of dog food, and the incense of fresh hay. You just knew farms, fields, and fishponds of boyhood couldn't be far away, but, alas, they were. Farmers negotiated their way to the old store past auto malls and warehouses, ultimately finding their familiar place farther than ever from sun-drenched fields shimmering with heat devils.

I loved going into this store because it revived memories of my farm adventures. I'd wander around looking at old implements and supplies—push plows on wheels, mule collars, mineral licks (we called them salt blocks), old fish mill cakes, white cucumber seeds, purple martin feeders, Ten Commandment lily bulbs, and even harnesses for cows. Hanging from a longleaf pine column were screen fly swatters for a mere $1.25.

On a wooden counter scratched deep with memories of past purchases sat a dignified, brass National cash register. Remember that familiar metallic clang of money exchanging hands? Nearby were automatic deer feeders, climbing tree stands, and 50-pound sacks of whole corn. An old poster of hunting dogs, pointers, overlooked sacks of dog food.

I found plenty of reminders of simper times here. No prepackaged seeds. Drawers of seeds instead, attended by scoops and scales, old-fashioned ways of measuring amounts. The scales, dented and tarnished, gauged tons of seeds over the decades. Those scales, like a veteran farmer, looked their age but remained accurate, as a Department of Agriculture accuracy certificate attested.

The flower seeds were headed for a classic destination: real clay pots, not plastic versions. Along a wall near the front door sat cardboard boxes and wooden crates of bare root bunches of collards and cabbages ready for planting.

Cases upon case of canned dog food were stacked in the aisles. Walking in a straight line was not possible, but that was okay. It forced me to look around a bit. And what did I see? Cedar bird feeders, sacks of birdseed, and a most curious device: a squirrel tormentor, sporting three blade-like props, each holding an ear of corn.

For the farmer who tired of rodents raiding his crop, the old store sold inflatable owls and snakes. The owls, in particular, were best sellers. And another bestseller was empty croaker sacks. For 95 cents you could buy an empty burlap sack and find endless uses for it. These croaker sacks held most anything, including frogs from a night of frog gigging, hence "croaker sack." Perhaps you've heard that fine Southern expression "I'd rather be buried in a croaker sack." I suspect some catty woman whispered that in church upon spying a rival all gussied up gaudy and glitzy.

The old feed and seed store also sold baby chicks. Many a preacher's Sunday meal originated from its dark redwood hatchery. That changed as more and more supermarkets sold processed fryers. And then one day, the hatchery incubated nothing but dust.

Hinson's Feed & Seed is no more. Where handwritten ads once hawked billy goats for $25 there was an Oriental rug place. Then it vanished. An art gallery came and went. Let enough time pass, and I imagine a bar will open there. Order a cold beer in the exact spot where hog ears and corn once found their way into paper sacks. Dance where mule collars hung.

Authentic feed and seed stores drop like flies, smitten by a screen swatter called progress. And the life I had as a boy adventuring around Granddad's farm? Well, that life exists only in the deep reaches of the country, for family farms melt away.

When I was a boy roaming the fields and pastures I held in my hands many things . . . cane poles, a carton of red wrigglers, warm eggs fresh with chicken mess, a stolen tomato, a string of fish, a big slice of watermelon, a BB gun, a slingshot, and a walking stick. Not one thing I carried required a battery.

I read that folks want the government to restrict the use of handheld electronic games, cell phones, pads, and tablets for kids. They want to help curb things like obesity and attention deficit disorder. When we were kids we had no problems like that thanks to the family farm. We got joy and a workout from the land itself. Keeping batteries charged? That was something Granddad did for his rusty but trusty International tractor.

CLOSED AT NOON WEDNESDAYS

Wednesday afternoons have long been sacred in small towns. Round about noon places close and the infamous slow Southern life style crawls to a stop. How did this custom begin? Nothing clearly explains how the tradition started, but a few theories are out there.

Farmers would come to town Saturdays to buy supplies and transact business. Stores opened half a day Saturdays to accommodate the farmers. It was the week's biggest payday.

Wednesday was a night for church and prayer meetings, and years ago a big dinner around 5:30 preceded the evening service. Folks needed time to cook and get ready for church.

Another explanation is the fact that stockyards had their big auctions Wednesday afternoons and anyone with market-ready cattle headed to the stockyard. Put all three together and you have good reason to take the afternoon off.

Still, after reading these reasons I still wasn't sure why Wednesday ended up being "the day." I appealed to my Georgialina readers for answers. Here's what others have to say.

McCormick South Carolina's Bob Edmonds: "In farm-based towns in the early times merchants were open 12 to 14 hours on Saturday. The Wednesday afternoon closing gave them a break."

Lincolnton, Georgia's Daryl Bentley, said, "I was always told by Dad that small town communities enjoyed Saturday as the main business day when country folk came to town for their shopping. Taking a half of a day Wednesday prevented businesses from having to work six full days a week."

Brenda Holloway Sanders of Lincolnton said, "I always thought things closed on Wednesday because of the cattle sales in Washington and something about bankers having to be there to approve money for the purchases."

Carol Nabers: "When I was younger, Newberry closed at noon on Wednesday afternoons." Author and Rome, Georgia, native Batt Humphreys grew up in Shelby, North Carolina. He offers an explanation I've heard more than a few times: "It was all a construct of the doctors and bankers to get tee times and play golf mid-week, at least, in my small town."

Having an afternoon off had to make the week pass easier for workers. As for shoppers, it was something that was just accepted and no one complained. Not so today. I overheard a person from up North griping about life in a rural outpost. "Apparently it's a Southern thing to close stores, banks, and utility companies Wednesday afternoon. Let me tell you it's mighty inconvenient if you're not used to it."

In *Lost in the Cosmos: The Last Self-Help Book*, Walker Percy, writing about a small town, said, "Home may be where the heart is but it's no place to spend Wednesday afternoon." Percy was born in Alabama and lived in Louisiana, but his words better suit transplants.

It wasn't a bother unless you didn't plan ahead. Back in the 1950s and 1960s we all knew the stores would lock doors come high noon. Not so today. Things are changing. In some small towns you can shop Wednesdays. Blame the chain stores. Blame malls and blame the Internet's online shopping. Blame a bad economy. I can tell you though that we need Wednesday afternoons off.

Laverne Story of San Antonio, a reader with family connections to my hometown, wrote me. "Having Lincolnton shut down every

Wednesday afternoon was always an endearing oddity to me. That was something unheard of in Maryland where we lived and was something my brother and I associated with Georgia, in addition to old houses and barns, red dirt roads, wood stoves and outhouses."

She continued, writing, "I thought it was interesting you quoted my first cousin, Darryl Bentley, who said his father gave the businessman's point of view. I always thought it was so Aunt Ruby could go shopping in Augusta! I'm sure there was a mass migration from Lincoln County on Wednesday afternoons by the majority of housewives. Ask your mother."

And then she wrote that she "laughed out loud" when she saw the City Pharmacy's advertisement "Now OPEN UNTIL 5 P.M. ON WEDNESDAYS" on the same page as my column "Closed at Noon Wednesdays."

I hate to see my hometown turning its back on this custom. I say keep Wednesday afternoons sacred. Consider it a gift. So, what can you do with a free afternoon every Wednesday? Plenty. Take care of things around the homestead. Visit family. Devote time to a secret longing: paint, write, study photography, learn to play the harmonica, do something, anything, constructive. Or . . . do nothing. Rest.

I fear small towns—those strongholds of "Closed Wednesdays"—will see this fine tradition fade as stores chase the almighty dollar and yet another part of the Southland slips away. I hope we keep the tradition alive.

For now, though, let's go back to a more civilized time, to a scene long repeated in places like Beaufort, South Carolina; Newberry, South Carolina; and a town called Lincolnton.

It's a hazy afternoon. The dog days of August are in full swing. Storm clouds crowd the horizon. As cicadas sing their summer song, the old courthouse clock starts to strike. As the twelfth stroke rings out, store lights go off and locks click shut. "Open" signs are turned to "Closed."

Streets and sidewalks empty. A few cars head out of town. One has old-fashioned cane fishing poles and a newfangled rod and reel sticking out the window. No storm will stop this old fisherman and his grandson. No sir. It's Wednesday afternoon, a bit of Saturday come early, a bit of midweek freedom that's priceless. And down on Soap

Creek they say the crappie are hitting Little Cleos and the bream, well, a cane pole and worms might catch a few.

·{ VANQUISHED }·
WAYS

The South's customs and traditions long set it apart from other regions. We've had and have some fine ways, though it's fashionable to criticize us for our ways. Well, that's all right. When you live in the best region, you're going to encounter jealousy and jibes.

Some old ways are vanishing, vanquished by progress. Take dowsing, which I know took place in other parts of the country. Other customs and traditions are disappearing thanks to progress and a powerful ally I'll disclose later. Here are a few ways we're losing what once seemed an indelible identity.

Dowsers

As a kid I remember seeing movies where some old codger would walk about with a Y-shaped twig called a diving rod. The rod would lead him about, and, despite his efforts to control it, down to the ground it'd point.

"There," the old water witch would exclaim. "Dig there."

A peach or willow branch with a fork made a better divining rod than branches from other trees, but it really didn't matter, as you'll see. I remember hearing about a fellow or two who could "find water." A dowser was a self-appointed expert, sort of like a witch doctor, and in ancient days some, in fact, viewed dowsers as sorcerers. Dowsing falls into a category akin to black magic, but in the days before well-drilling rigs came along you had to start somewhere.

When scientifically tested, dowsers fail. James Randi, a fellow who exposes flimflams, tested some dowsers using a process all agreed upon. If they could locate water in underground pipes at an 80 percent success rate they'd get $10,000. Good inducement but not good enough. All failed.

You could say dowsers are all wet. Besides, now that city water runs into the country it makes all this dowser business obsolete. Dowsers are about as necessary as guys delivering blocks of ice packed in sawdust.

Handheld Fans in Church

Staple a handle that looked like a big ice cream stick to a funeral home ad and behold you had the handheld fan. It was indispensable in a sweltering church during a long-winded sermon. Often these fans portrayed Jesus with his arms outspread. A cross upon a hill with a dramatic sky as a backdrop was often used, and come Easter I remember seeing lilies on fans.

No self-respecting society woman was without her fan when a hot and humid Sunday rolled around. I remember seeing a stately lady pull out her collapsible fan one Sunday at New Hope. It was black with white flowers on it. She fanned herself in a haughty way. Sure, it would cool you, but it was also a status symbol, and then central air-conditioning relegated handheld fans to mere memories. Today, a woman with a yearning to be a cut above others has to find another status symbol. Try diamonds, dear.

Casting Spells to Remove Warts

An old fellow wearing a straw hat with a green sunshade rid me of a pesky wart. He was at Dad's shop getting something fixed. He rubbed a piece of broomstraw over the wart while muttering an incantation. He broke the straw in half and told me to go into the woods and throw that half over my left shoulder and never look at it again. I did as he said and a month or so later, the wart was gone.

Now we just buy a bottle of Dr. Scholl's Wart Remover or let a doctor freeze it off. That's cool but nowhere as cool as a wart spell.

Sitting with the Dead

Another tradition rarely practiced is sitting up all night with the dead. In the old days, someone sat by the dearly departed until the body was lowered into its eternal resting place. For one thing, folks back then couldn't be sure the person was dead. If, for whatever miraculous reason, the dead soul stirred, someone would be there to save the person from a funeral. For another thing, many funeral homes were too small to accommodate the crowd that convened to pay their respects. Yet another reason was to shoo away rats. (Yes, I know what you're thinking. Where was d-CON?)

Advanced medicine killed this tradition. The departed spend their last night on earth alone, sad to say. In a closely related vein, neither do you hear church bells in the country tolling once the hearse comes into sight. The mournful peal of the tolling bell leaves the air quieter and, alas, poorer. Without that tolling bell, John Donne's Meditation no. 17, "Devotions upon Emergent Occasions" doesn't resonate as it should: "No man is an island, entire of itself; every man is a piece of the continent, a part of the main. If a clod be washed away by the sea, Europe is the less, as well as if a promontory were, as well as if a manor of thy friend's or of thine own were: any man's death diminishes me, because I am involved in mankind, and therefore never send to know for whom the bell tolls; it tolls for thee." And cows!

Cowbells

Mom remembers how cowbells blessed the air with a melodic tinkling as cows grazed in distant pastures. No one places cowbells around cows' necks today that I know of. It'd be a peaceful, beautiful thing to hear cowbells ringing. As that infamous skit went on *Saturday Night Live* with Christopher Walken, we need "more cowbell."

Divining rods, hand fans, sitting all night with the dead, removing warts with straw, and the refrain of church bells and cowbells all have something in common. Not one relies on electricity, that nefarious ally of progress. The next time you lose power to a summer storm, you'll be transported to those old days and old ways in an instant. Maybe you'll sit up all night waiting for the electricity. Maybe you'll fan yourself as the heat climbs . . . if you can find a fan.

Younger folks and outsiders often think losing traditions is good, but I disagree. As we lose traditions, we lose touch with our past, and, if nothing else, a lot of traditions and customs made the good old days special. Settling for a bland, homogeneous world leads to a monotonous world. And that's not a tradition as much as it is a concession, and a bad one at that.

The mile-a-minute vine that ate Georgialina knows no barriers.
This import from southern Japan and southeast China covers old trucks,
abandoned homes, powerlines—anything and everything.

PHOTOGRAPH BY ROBERT C. CLARK

A LAND
TRANSFORMED

When Savannah River Site locked up 310 square miles of South Carolina, it created the eastern United States' single largest restricted area. In a Cold War paradox Savannah River Site guaranteed that this mammoth area would never be developed. People are restricted from coming here, and that makes it a natural area like few others. But it came with a price. Just ask the people who made an exodus from a place called Ellenton.

Kudzu, an exotic, established itself as part of the South's mystique. It stopped erosion, all right, but it covers forests and anything else in its path today. Meanwhile the land continues to reel under the assault of progress. It's rare to see fire towers and windmills. Cell towers that look like Martians from H. G. Wells's *War of the Worlds* are taking their place.

And that romantic lane, the dusty dirt road long ago surrendered to the god Asphalt. A rain-splattered asphalt road has nowhere the earthy fragrance a dirt road has.

Even sea creatures suffer a changing land. Sea turtles need all the help they can get. Way too many dune lines surrendered to development. Human activity has changed so much of the South. They say old rice plantations used as much labor as building the pyramids. Slaves left a beautiful if controversial legacy. And humanity's adverse influence even reached out to pristine islands where DDT almost did away with shorebirds. The land changes, but we remember how things used to be.

·{ ATOMIC }· PARADISE

I was stocking shelves with canned soup at Mr. Clifford's country store earning 25 cents an hour when a man said, "Yeah, he got a job at the bum plant."

"He," I figured, "must be a hobo," and I imagined a place where drifters worked, which meant they weren't bums after all. As the Cold War escalated, a teacher discussed Los Alamos, and the prettiest girl in class, Peggy, described her dad's fallout shelter. Like a flash, it hit me. "Bomb plant."

In what seemed an unimaginable distance away to a ten-year-old, workers, scientists, military experts, and weaponry wizards were refining the material that could annihilate Russia. The bomb plant was near Aiken—a 61-mile drive from home. Then I discovered that the woman next door, Miss Ann, made the 120-plus-mile roundtrip five days a week. A peacekeeper of sorts, she'd gotten on at the bum plant and made things hoboes could only dream about.

For a long time I knew little about this nuclear reservation.

Years passed.

One July day in 1986 a self-assigned writing project took me to Savannah River Site, the place of childhood hoboes. And what a site! Larger than my home county by 53 square miles, the site sprawled, then as now, over 310 square miles. Its ravenous radiation-fed appetite consumed communities, farmland, graveyards, and a town. The government moved Ellenton lock, stock, and barrel outside the site, a disruptive event like few others.

A hand-lettered sign at the city limits expressed the evicted peoples' sentiment: "It is hard to understand why our town must be destroyed to make a bomb that will destroy someone else's town that they love as much as we love ours. But we feel that they picked not just the best spot in the US, but in the world."

That July afternoon when I first saw Ellenton, brushy undergrowth grew where homes had sat. Where people once slept vines hung from trees. Curbs still looked solid. Not so the cracking sidewalks, which lay beneath a veneer of grass. The school's playground resisted nature's efforts to reclaim what is hers. Years of small feet running and jumping, playing ball, Red Rover Red Rover, and tag had packed the soil into an impermeable surface.

Many of the younger residents who left never returned. Of those 50 or older who relocated to New Ellenton, more than half died within a decade. Expatriates forbidden to visit their old homes, their will to live withered. Neither were the dead spared. One hundred and fifty graveyards were relocated to a *real* eternal rest. The people from Ellenton who capitulated? In surrendering their town they saved the homes of people across the world, but the radiation? It's alive and well.

People just can't be at this place anymore. This fact and the need for security keep everyday people persona non grata, making the site a natural laboratory, a coup the University of Georgia scored in 1951. Boars, bobcats, perhaps bears, deer, and other wild things dwell in this region of shutdown reactors. The ecology lab's mission was to study radiation's effect on plants, animals, and simple-celled organisms. It sounded like a good story to tell.

That July afternoon, on a nature quest in the belly of an atomic beast, I began to write. The Ecology Lab's director, Whit Gibbons, guided me around. He took me to a large creek, a small river in fact that steamed from waters that had just cooled reactors' cores. I walked onto a steep bank. At its base steam rose over boulders lacquered in orange algae. "Martian," I thought, "looks just like Mars." On both sides of this river-creek stood the ghostly tops of dead trees, a scene out of *Terminator.* I wanted to draw my fingers through that water to gauge its heat. As I squatted to do just that, the pine straw beneath me rolled and I slid feet first toward the water. Whit grabbed me just before my feet plunged into the water.

"Man, I'm glad you caught me," I said, much relieved.

"Me, too," he said, even more relieved. "If you had fallen in I would have been filling out paperwork for weeks."

On one occasion, we drove by massive terraces guarded by razor wire, the burial site for "hot" material with a 100,000-year lifespan. Among the concerns for this radioactive graveyard is the fear language might change so much over 100,000 years that people will forget what's here.

And on another assignment I saw a building like few others. "You aren't allowed to photograph that," said my guide, a wetlands ecologist. We were driving by a baleful building, R Reactor, the site's first production reactor. It once manufactured tritium and plutonium-239 isotopes. In 1963, after ten years of operation, a defective fuel rod released Cesium 137 into Par Pond, a manmade lake for cooling reactors. Months later, President Johnson called for a reduction in the arms race. R Reactor closed June 17, 1964. All these years later, looking at R Reactor amounts to a Cold War history lesson. For all we know it staved off global calamity.

In 2011 the powers that be decommissioned the reactor and filled it with cement, turning it into an impenetrable block. They welded its doors shut. It will stay this way for the next 1,400 years, a nanosecond to the cosmos.

Would I go back? Yes. But not to see R Reactor. I'd go to see the nation's first cloverleaf and Ellenton again. I'd stand inside a home's foundation and imagine the people who loved this empty space. Perhaps I'd smell biscuits baking, chicken frying, see a TV with rabbit ears facing a plaid sofa, and, just out the front window, a Plymouth with fins like a great white.

I will go back to this Atomic Diaspora where an unexpected exodus uprooted 6,000 people. I'll go back because seeing how easily lives can be changed humbles you. I'll go back because SRS is more natural than most places, save wildlife refuges and national parks, and in some ways it trumps those. Carolina bay wetlands and biological diversity ennoble this place. In a great paradox, a place that refined materials for hydrogen bombs created a grand oasis where more than 240 bird species, more than 100 species of reptiles and amphibians, and nearly 100 species of freshwater fish live. A creek coursing through here exhibits the greatest diversity of invertebrates of any creek in the Western Hemisphere. South Carolina's largest alligator—more than 13 feet long—lived here. As Gibbons pointed out in *USA Today*, "These are not nuclear mutants, simply specimens grown large because they are not hunted or fished. It's a pretty simple formula," he said. "The best protection for the environment is no people."

No people. It's a superb formula. Think how many buildings, parking lots, sewer systems, gas lines, power lines, convenience stores, golf courses, piles of garbage, and dumpsters would afflict these 310 square miles had no SRS existed. But it did, and instead you find solitude. The wind whispers through pines. You hear not one cry from civilization. No contrails, no aircraft mar the blemish-free sky. No litter. No billboards. No mowers. It's like going back 300 years . . . the way things used to be.

Miss Ann died of cancer. I remember seeing her lying in bed waiting for the end. Maybe radiation killed her. I doubt she realized the majesty surrounding her as she worked away, one of my childhood hoboes. She worked in a wildlife refuge but never spent one night there.

I, however, dream of camping in this atomic paradise. I'll set my camp in a grassy plain beneath stars undiluted by city lights and count shooting stars. I'll never get to do that, of course, and you'll never go to SRS without solid justification. As close as you will get is driving through on S.C. Highway 125 or taking a guided tour. The influence of people here just isn't what it once was, and that suits me fine.

·{ KUDZU EATS }·
{ THE SOUTH }

In Georgia, the legend says
that you must close your window

at night to keep it out of the house.
The glass is tinged with green, even so
James Dickey, "Kudzu"

Give thanks that Lowe's and Home Depot don't sell kudzu. What a mess we'd be in if they did. Imagine seeing a plant that grows a foot a day everywhere you go. Out in the country kudzu has long eaten the South, and if you sit still as a stone near a mound of kudzu you can hear it growing. It sounds like Saran wrap being pulled taut. Spreading for many miles, it reaches out and curls its tentacles around anything in its path.

Kudzu mounds up over the land, a green creature that devours all. When I see a forest covered by this tree-eating plant, I hate to speculate what's inside all that tangled greenery. It seems to be the perfect place to hide a body.

Over the years it's occurred to me that kudzu and junkyards share an affinity for each other. I read where men discovered classic cars swallowed whole by kudzu in Alabama. Hacking away with machetes, men uncovered a 1967 Camaro and a 1972 Grand Torino. The men walked on top of kudzu-covered cars having no idea what was beneath their feet. In time they liberated a 1967 Lincoln Continental. Kudzu, nothing stops it.

A lot of forests and farmland vanished into that leafy green sea some call the cancer of the plant world. By preventing trees from getting sunlight, it starves them to death. Growing a foot a day, it blankets trees, power poles, fences, yards, houses, cars, trucks—anything in its path. It is one of few invaders that are closely identified with the South. It has done what armadillos, hydrilla, coyotes, and some Northern folks have not managed to do: become a cultural icon.

The pesky vine keeps making inroads into our culture. Near Elberton, Georgia folks named a road for it. That means even GPS devices must accommodate kudzu. Everything from restaurants to comic strips to rock bands has been named for the plant. Poets, as you see, have written about it. Down in Tallahassee, Florida, at Florida State they produce a literary journal called *The Kudzu Review*.

Humid, blistering days and sweaty nights provide near-perfect conditions for kudzu's rampages. Winters are mild with few hard freezes, the humidity is high, and ample rain falls. Kudzu grows better here than it does in its native land of Japan. No wonder it covers more than 7 million acres in the South.

It's difficult to eradicate. Years and years of herbicide don't make a dent in it, and in fact it has grown even faster after being treated by some herbicides. Its roots can reach 12 feet deep and weigh up to 500 pounds.

When I was a boy we had a tough patch of honeysuckle in the back yard. To kill it we put my Granddad Poland's goats back there, and they chewed it into oblivion. Kudzu isn't so easily banished. Kudzu has no natural predators, although I wonder what legions of goats or sheep might do to it.

If you can't get rid of it, you might as well use it. Granddad Walker strung hemp from column to column on his front porch and planted kudzu at its base. Kudzu would climb that latticework, providing privacy and shade come the dog days of August. I have fond memories of hiding behind that green screen of vegetation. It filtered sunlight to a soft green and it felt like the temperature dropped 20 degrees when you sat in a rocker behind that infamous plant brought here to stem the wearing away of the Southland.

The 1876 Philadelphia Centennial Exposition hyped kudzu as a decorative plant and a way to control erosion. *Time* would list kudzu's introduction to the United States as one of the 100 worst ideas of the twentieth century.

People believed this import would solve erosion problems. Instead of deep red gullies they saw green vines. The champion of kudzu was Covington, Georgia's Channing Cope. He envisioned the conversion of "wastelands" into kudzu pastures. That was the message he hammered through in his daily radio programs and *Atlanta Journal-Constitution* articles.

He started the Kudzu Club of America in the early 1940s. By 1943, 20,000 people had joined. The club's goal was to plant a million acres of kudzu in Georgia and 8 million acres in the South. Cope compared the planting of kudzu on heavily eroded land to a physician's use of medicine to fight a disease.

In an ironic twist, some say kudzu killed Cope. Cope's friend Philip S. Cohen said that even after the government labeled the vine an ecological threat, Cope would not let the county cut back the profusion of kudzu on his land. The kudzu was so thick it enclosed the road leading to his home, Yellow River Plantation. Teenagers saw the dense kudzu as a haven, a place to park and party. When Cope tried to run off these adolescent interlopers one evening, he walked three feet and fell dead from a massive heart attack.

Now we're stuck with the plant Cope championed. In "Kudzu: A Tale of Two Vines," an essay published in *Southern Cultures*, the academic researchers Derek Alderman and Donna Alderman wrote, "Southerners both endure and embrace this pervasive part of life. Some wage an ecological battle against kudzu, while others use and market the vine in creative ways. . . . As a national news wire reports, 'So aggressive is kudzu that the word has entered American English as shorthand for out-of-control growth.'"

The plant has one merit at least. Kudzu's long clusters of dark-purple flowers bloom mostly in July and August. Mom tells me they give off a pleasant smell, like grapes. The next time I see kudzu and it's in bloom, I'll check it out. I'll proceed with care. Said Lewis Grizzard, "Nothing grows faster than a kudzu vine. It has been known to cover entire homes in Georgia where the families are asleep for the night. They are then trapped inside and can't get to a convenience store, so they starve. Those who try to eat their way out of kudzu quickly have their innards entangled in the vine because no matter how much you chew it, the blamed stuff just keeps on growing."

A joke goes that a Yankee asked a Southern farmer how to grow kudzu. (As if it needs help.) The farmer tells the Yankee to stomp on the ground a few times to get its attention, throw the kudzu seeds on the ground, then run like there's no tomorrow.

Well, there is a tomorrow for kudzu. The plant that's eating the South never goes on a diet. It's here to stay. As the poem advises, if you live near a forest of kudzu, keep your windows closed at night.

·{ THE LAST DIRT ROAD }·

One summer, rain was scarce. Something about drought makes me think of dirt roads. When the land bakes and the barest winds stir, I' see billowing clouds of dust trailing a car down a dirt lane back of Mr.

Clifford's store. A dark sedan flies toward me, a contrail of powdery dust coating everything, me included. I can taste it, earthy and dry. Then saliva turns it to mud and I spit it back whence it came, a dirt road. That dusty lane is paved now.

Some day, somewhere, the South will have one last dirt road. "It's getting hard," said Robert Clark, "to find dirt roads." We were discussing another photo-essay book on South Carolina we were authoring for the University of South Carolina Press. We were looking over photographs when we came across a photo of a dirt road, an endangered species and another aspect of the South that's fading away. We still have classic dirt roads. One of Georgialina's finest is on Edisto Island. This road, framed by live oaks festooned with Spanish moss and resurrection ferns, possesses an exotic name, Botany Bay Road.

Dirt roads bring a romantic touch to fiction. I can't recall reading a description of a paved road in literature. They're just not interesting. Hemingway painted a beautiful portrait of a dirt road in *A Farewell to Arms:*

> In the late summer of that year we lived in a house in a village
> that looked across the river and the plain to the mountains. . . .
> Troops went by the house and down the road and the dust they
> raised powdered the leaves of the trees. The trunks of the trees
> too were dusty and the leaves fell early that year and we saw the
> troops marching along the road and the dust rising and leaves,
> stirred by the breeze, falling and the soldiers marching and
> afterward the road bare and white except for the leaves.

There's something poetic about a dirt road. Now we insist on paving every road we can. Some of you are thinking, "Yeah, well, maybe you've never been mired to the axles on a dirt road turned into a quagmire by rain." I have been stuck on a dirt road turned into a sea of mud. When I was a boy my family drove over to Carolina to see my mom's brother. When we left it was raining, and the car got stuck. Dad had me get out and push. I remember riding back to Georgia covered in mud. That was eons ago, and I am certain that road is paved today.

Back when roads were lanes made from whatever the earth offered, everyone was on equal, if slippery, footing. Then gravel and tar came along. If you lived on a paved road you had a bit of status. Those left to deal with dust and mud were jealous. But you had no dust, no mud, just the ding of gravel against the undercarriage, and then asphalt came along, a mix of crude oils and aggregate, and people everywhere wanted their road paved.

A washboard lane makes a car skitter about, and sooner or later potholes will develop. Sufficient reason to lay down asphalt. What beauty we lose, though. On my drive down I-20 to home, I used to see a dirt road winding through the pines not far from Graniteville. One day I came along and it had been paved. The vista no longer holds the same interest, and I never glance that way anymore.

As a boy I loved seeing a big yellow road grader planing off a veneer of dirt, curls of clay gathering at the ends of its blade. You could smell the earth's raw fertility as the grader rid the road of potholes and washboard ridges. The cycle was welcomed. Inevitably the grader would return to smooth a weathered road. I recall the shock I felt at seeing a familiar road covered with tar and gravel. Each road that surrendered to an artificial surface gave up the feeling of a rural past. Once the paving began it didn't stop. A politician never met a road he didn't want to pave.

Is it in fact a sign of progress when a dirt road gets paved? We show our dependency on petroleum, and when cracks, holes, and wear take their toll, we lay down another layer of asphalt. Taxes, maintenance, and other issues such as speeding become a nuisance. Potholes, ruts, and ridges, you see, serve as a kind of law enforcement. Speeding down a dirt road isn't a lot of fun; certainly it's no good for your shocks and struts.

I hear though that dirt roads cost twice as much to maintain as paved roads. Even so, can we not spare a few dirt roads a heavy layer of asphalt? Why not let unpaved roads remind ensuing generations that this is how things used to be? Let them discover that it just feels better to drive down a road that no white and yellow paint can ever stain.

I hear folks buying resort homes see dirt roads as evocative of more pastoral times. These supporters of earlier times believe dirt roads are safer. Folks have no choice but to drive slower.

Dirt roads slow development, too. Can't build dream homes subject to dust and mud, can we? More than anything, people enjoy the rustic appearance of dirt roads and the feeling of being transported back in time. When a cloud comes up and those first drops spatter against a dirt road they'll get a rich smell that's the smell of life itself. They'll never get that from a paved road. What they will get is more traffic, more development, and more noise.

ALONG THE DUNE LINE

Long ago I wrote a film script about a subject most people give little thought to: sand dunes. The stars of this natural history documentary were sea oats, pelicans, shorebirds, and loggerhead sea turtles. The goal? Show people how important sand dunes are to wildlife and humanity. Because of scheduling issues and bad weather, *Sand Dunes: Guardian of the Coast* hit the screen without its true stars. And then career changes got in the way. It took a book project, 33 years, and a twist of fate to see the end of my own story.

Nesting season was almost spent. It was late August, 10:15 in the evening on Cape Island, the outermost island in Cape Romain National Wildlife Refuge. Above this wild island the heavens wheel and night takes on incomparable majesty. The sky pulsates with brilliant stars. Meteors streak the sky. The luminous surf falls, scattering phosphorescent foam across a silver beach. You see no signs of civilization. All you hear are the wind and the rhythmic surge of water. It's far more than the rising and subsiding of white noise. It's Earth inhaling and exhaling. Nature rules here. It is an ideal place to film wildlife for a simple reason. People have yet to ruin it.

I was there to film our next-to-last scene, a loggerhead sea turtle laying eggs along the dune line. For hours we patrolled the beach, scanning the milky surf to spot the head of a female who pauses at the surf line to check for predators.

To find a turtle on the nest is ideal, and you do that by sitting still and every so often looking for turtle tracks. If you find a place where it looks like someone has dragged a desk up to the dune line, you're in business. And so, like some cats out of a Johnny Cash song, we walked the line into the wee hours but saw not one sign of a turtle.

Eleven, midnight, one, two . . . the hours crawled by; turtles did not. At 3 A.M. we were ready to give up. Facing a long cruise through the estuary and more than two hours' driving to Columbia, we decided to make one more sweep down the beach. And then we saw it. A fresh scrape mark. When you come across a scrape you have to give the turtle time to dig a nest and start laying. Once she begins laying you can set up lights and film away. She won't budge until the last egg drops.

After a reasonable wait we walked up to a massive dune where a turtle was dropping eggs into a hole. She must have weighed 300 pounds. Barnacles and other sea creatures had hitched a ride on her carapace, and she smelled earthy, organic, a mix of salt and sulfur. The filming went well and we left, resolving to return and film baby turtles scrambling out of the nest and making their way to the sea. We knew that in 55 to 60 days her clutch of 120 or so eggs would hatch out. We'd come back when the spartina was golden and the winds bit. That was the plan.

Problem is I never came back to see the baby turtles claw out of the sand and make their way to the cresting Atlantic. It was something that always gnawed at me.

A lifetime passed, and at last I saw what I had missed so long ago. I had the privilege of observing a team of volunteers, among them Mary Pringle, the project leader for sea turtle nest protection on Isle of Palms and Sullivan's Island. Robert Clark and I had a rendezvous at Sullivan's Island set up by the *New York Times* best-selling author Mary Alice Monroe. We were there to photograph Mary Alice and the turtle team as they inventoried nests to see how many turtles had hatched.

Why the big deal over loggerhead sea turtles? Simple. A major headache for loggerhead sea turtles is finding nesting habitat. Coastal development, predation, folks wandering beaches with flashlights, and accidental capture by commercial fishing vessels all take a toll on turtle populations. The little tykes need all the help they can get.

7:30 on a balmy August evening. A soft summer evening isn't the worst time to liberate baby turtles. For one thing the sand isn't as hot. For another, evening is nigh and darkness increases their chance of evading predators.

Wearing latex gloves and a blue turtle team t-shirt and cap, Mary Alice carefully dug into a nest. A mix of hatchlings and spent eggs came out slowly. Hatchlings went into a bucket. When all the hatchlings were accounted for, all the eggs, hatched or not, went back into the nest and were covered up.

Mary Alice's nest gave up 14 babies; all went into a fire-engine-red bucket. A team member drew two lines in the sand, the corridor down which the baby turtles would crawl seaward. No one could cross these lines. The bucket of babies was gently laid over, and out scrambled the latest generation of sea turtles. Toward the water they went. The odds weren't good. Just one in every 1,000 babies will make it to adulthood. Fourteen turtles is a sobering number. When the last baby turtle slipped beneath a small wave, the worrying began.

When *Caretta caretta*, as the loggerhead's scientific name goes, enters the sea, it becomes a mystery for ten years or more. Experts believe loggerheads live for 60 or more years. No one knows a whole lot about the turtles until they grow to "plate" size.

It was exciting and a bit sobering to see the baby turtles slip beneath the Atlantic one by one. When the waves wash over them they're on their own and all we can do is to wish them luck. The last scene in *Sand Dunes: Guardians of the Coast* was to do just this: show baby sea turtles making their way to the surf line. There the waves would toss them back time and time again, but, resolute, they'd persist until the sea accepted them. Closing credits would crawl over this timeless struggle. By now, though, you know that scene went wanting.

It was 35 years ago when I filmed the nesting turtle on Cape Island, and since 30 years must pass before a female matures and can lay eggs of her own, I'm curious. Did the one in a 1,000 survivor of those eggs I filmed lay the eggs Mary Alice so carefully handled? The turtles that just slipped into the sea—were they the grandchildren of the turtle I filmed so long ago? It's a slim chance but not out of the realm of possibility. "Natal homing" holds that a turtle will nest within 5 to 35 miles of where she herself hatched, and Cape Island is pretty close as the turtle swims.

The film, in my mind, was complete. And the hatchlings? They faced much adversity. I hope fate gave them every break possible.

·{ CAROLINA GOLD }·

Early one spring I went to rice-field country near Georgetown and Mansfield Plantation. The moment I turned off Highway 701 onto Mansfield Road I hurtled 300 years into the past. I saw the Old South that struggled in dead teachers' arid classrooms begin to come alive.

I saw the antebellum South and once-endangered wildlife. I saw osprey and two flocks of American white pelicans overwintering from Alberta and Northwest Territories. Bald eagles whistled and wheeled above a distant field as I walked toward the allée of oaks Mel Gibson rode through in *The Patriot*.

I saw vestiges of a 300-year-old-old rice plantation. One word comes to mind: sumptuous. Dogwood bracts flecked Spanish moss with white. Dogwood's tender, just-minted leaves—emerald snow-flakes—burst with life. Vines and resurrection ferns hitched rides to nowhere on broad live oak limbs. And why should they care to go anywhere? They dwell in perfection. Azalea and camellia blossoms fought head to head for my eyes, and the broad sweep of this flatland gives them ample battleground. I saw an old joggling board, too, Charleston green. The Old South, the one that placed avenues of oaks on vinegar bottles, lives here.

There's an old ruin here, the smokestack that ran the old rice mill machinery. Beyond it stands a drained impoundment. The cool spring, sunlight has worked it over good. A tile fitter could set tiles the color of creamed coffee alongside the cracked, tessellated earth and you wouldn't notice the difference.

The construction of rice impoundments and the growing and harvesting of rice were labor-intensive efforts that have been compared to the building of the pyramids. Leftovers from the work remain . . . dikes, rice fields, slave cabins, and a strange building high on stilts—the country's last winnowing barn.

Millions of pounds of Carolina Gold passed through the winnowing barn at Mansfield. First women had to pound it for hours. In the barn they shook it loose and swept it into cracks in the floor. Slipping through the cracks, the grains tumbled into a muslin tarp attached to the stilts—an immense sack, if you will. The chaff? Gone with the wind, and out went the rice to feed the world.

Walking down the allée of oaks, my back to the Black River, I come to the slave cabins. Inside one cabin an old door painted haint blue leans against a corner. "Haint" is Gullah for "haunt." Haint blue wards off bad spirits. It's said that dirt daubers won't build nests on anything painted haint blue. Must be true. I saw no "dobber" nests. A fireplace splattered haint blue with double hearths stood in the middle of this cabin. Two families—or two groups—lived here at a time.

Overhanging the cabin, old oak limbs point across a sandy lane to the chapel. Poignant beauty lives in that old chapel's simple lines, old wood, ancient bricks, and cedar shake roof. Simple pine benches face the pulpit. The singsong sermons that rang out here must have been something . . . the shouts and songs, too.

> Before I'd be a slave, I'd be buried in my grave, And go home
>   to my Lord, And be saved
> O, what preachin'! O, what preachin'! O what preachin'!

At the end of the chapel by the chimney stands a bell tower. The old bell, freckled with rust, is quiet, its clapper still. A wooden sign is displayed beneath the old chapel bell. It reads exactly as I have it here: "o lord prop us up in all our leaning places" (from Archibald Rutledge, *God's Children*, 1947).

I stayed 'til dark taking in the haunting beauty of this 1718 plantation. As a bald eagle wheeled and cried out, a rich diversity of bird life responded. Last call before roosting time. Brown grasses rattled beneath a cold wind sweeping off the Black River. Winter still held the land, but spring was prying its fingers loose. Darkness set in, and I called it a day.

Dawn at Mansfield. Mists drift through the oaks and if I look across the grounds just so, no latter-day trappings mar the view. Just marsh, water, oaks, and moss. A rosy patina glazes the eastern horizon. Foggy, surreal marshscapes rise from the past. Work chants ring out across rice fields.

A chorus of birdsong builds as pileated woodpeckers' tapping punctuates the concert. It must have been like this in Carolina Gold's heyday, only richer with waterfowl.

A vast fortune passed through sights and sounds such as these. Some rice planters made a million dollars a year. Prosperity reigned, and then the Civil War came calling and a hurricane pushed salt water into the rice fields, further ruining things.

Relics from the glory days remain. Here's a pile of old bricks heaped against the base of an oak. Really old bricks. When planet Earth dies, among civilization's wreckage will be bricks. You can break a brick, but you can't kill it. Early light softens these old bricks, giving them a sheen born of weathering. It's as if satin covers them. A few bricks are rounded at each end. They came over as ship ballast in wooden ships driven by the winds, but there's little wind before dawn. Not yet.

Earth's rotation serves up the gift of life. Showering gold, boiling incandescent gases—the nearest star breaks over the Black. Diamonds glint on the river and gossamer gold overlays the land. The deep-green crowns of yesterday's live oaks gleam with lemony luster. No white pelicans are about but were they, they too would be gold.

An easterly zephyr arrives and the Spanish moss dances. Soon the wind stiffens and drapes of Spanish moss swing to the west.

The day asserts itself. The mists evaporate and normalcy returns.

People come to savor the Old South. In the parking lot I see license plates from up north. I'm not sure if they understand how places like Mansfield came to be. All the rice that came from here and other plantations fed a lot of people. The demand was there. It took a lot of labor to mine that gold. It took something else. Innovation and a certain mix of water.

Rather than plant rice inland in swamps, visionary planters turned to tidal cultivation. A lowcountry tidal river had to mix with brackish water just so. If a river carried a sheet of freshwater on its surface as the sea backed it inland, all was fine. All that was needed were ways to control the flow. Rice trunks—ingenious devices made of cypress— did just that. (At first inland swamp rice planters laughed at them. They didn't laugh long.)

Rice dikes, dams, and trunks did the trick. One slave could now produce 3,000 to 3,600 pounds of rice—five or six times the yield per slave from inland swamps. The way to grow rice changed, but in the end it all was for naught.

As I near the end you might suppose I'm going to to blast the past. But I can't take responsibility for the past. I'll leave the criticism of it to those who dissect the past for a living. Was slavery inhumane? Of course.

Driving back to the Midlands, I am haunted by images of the grand old plantation. I tried to come up with words that capture the essence of the Old South's rice-field remnants. The best I could do was this: old bricks, red camellias, lost glories, hard labor, suffering, green al-lées, flaming azaleas, singsong sermons, chants, and moody flats of water salted by strangely white pelicans.

FOR THE BIRDS

For three summers running in the 1960s, I spent two weeks at my aunt's home in Summerville. Daily trips to Folly Beach made my heart beat wildly. All that openness, sun, sea, and stretches of beach created a horizon like no other. I could see for miles.

When I went back home to eastern Georgia's forests and hills, the world closed in on me, and a longing for salt, sand, and spray consumed me. Nothing's worse than growing up landlocked once you've had a taste of the sea.

Rural outposts grow big dreams in country boys and my dream was to live on the coast. Fate, however, had something else in mind—something *beyond* the coast—beautiful islands in a beautiful refuge called Cape Romain.

In 1978 I applied for a job as a scriptwriter/cinematographer for natural history films. I got the job. For a deliciously brief time, I visited the wild islands of Cape Romain Wildlife Refuge.

Even a sorry photographer knows the best light is at dawn. Up at 2 A.M., I would race the sun to the coast, the light falling in my wake on haunted, green swamps and oaks dripping with Spanish moss. The stars told me I was moving deeper into the land of blackwater rivers and white sands, so deep my journey would take me to the jumping-off place, a landing at McClellanville.

My first crossing was one to remember. In predawn darkness, we put out in a Boston Whaler crewed by U.S. Fish and Wildlife Service boatman Herbert Manigault. The Whaler's engine hummed as we made our way through the estuary to one of the last wild islands, Bull Island. About 300 yards from the marshy side, Herbert killed the engine. The unceasing sound of 10,000 Dewalt drills piercing steel crossed the water—mosquitoes by the millions.

I didn't care. I felt as if I were about to step onto the shores of Africa. And I felt this way for three summers in Cape Romain, a refuge that wraps barrier islands and salt marsh habitats around 22 miles of Atlantic coast. The refuge holds 35,267 acres of beach and sand dunes, salt marsh, maritime forests, tidal creeks, fresh and brackish water impoundments, and 31,000 acres of open water. Nature rules. It is an ideal place to film wildlife for a simple reason: people have yet to ruin it.

Orange-billed oystercatchers and white egrets vibrate against green spartina. Chocolate pluff mud that hints of sulfur counterbalances gritty beaches. Creeks are blue arteries that loop, double back, and nourish the green-gold spartina. The sea-ravaged maritime forest, however, leaves you breathless.

Every time I approached Bull Island, D-Day came to mind. Root-balls of live oaks, loblolly pine, and cabbage palmetto litter the beach like the Czech hedgehogs and log ramps Germans planted on Omaha Beach. It looks like a battle scene, and it's a battle the trees lost.

Toppled trees, their sun-bleached limbs white as marble, lie strewn about, monuments to the moon and its tides. Stripped of foliage and bark and smoothed by sand and sea, the trees are about the end of things. Even death is beautiful in the islands.

Clamoring shorebirds swirl overhead, dropping bombs that necessitate wearing long sleeves and caps. (Never look straight up when you're in a rookery.)

The cup of life overflows here. The islands, pristine, sun splashed, and desolate, truly are for the birds because desolation is where the business of raising fledglings best takes place. Though sandpipers, plovers, oystercatchers, ruddy turnstones, laughing gulls, and scores of feathered species live here, my trips to Cape Romain involved pelicans, sand dunes, and sea turtles.

Imagine clouds of birds flying over a mosaic of straw-stick nests filled with eggs and purple dollops. That's what a pelican colony looks like. Amid this clamorous collage, I trained my Arriflex on fledgling pelicans, featherless, brownish-purple blobs. A rookery of jiggling fledglings is a dizzying thing. Many die, and the sun-ripened smell overpowers you. But I liked the little rascals. I knew they were overcoming a hard time.

DDT's runoff from farm fields into rivers and then the sea put a hurt on the eastern brown pelican and other bird species. Plankton absorbed DDT, menhaden ate plankton, and pelicans ate menhaden in a game of food-chain dominoes that reduced the pelican eggs' calcium content. Thin and easily crushed, the flawed eggs put the pelican on the endangered-species list in the early 1970s. The ban on DDT and recovery efforts saved the pelicans.

Least terns deserve at least a mention because they shared nesting space with the pelicans. A scrape in the sand just above the waterline—that's where least terns nest. Their eggs, tan with brown specks, look like sand. They're near invisible.

Today, least terns here and there colonize the graveled rooftops of buildings, commentary on how we've destroyed nesting habitat and another reason I love Cape Romain. Its feathery alchemy transforms sand scrapes into the seashore's grand aviary.

It was hot. There was no shade, just sun, sand, sky, and sea. The sun bears down on eggs destined to fill the sky in a great cycle of feathers, feeding, and seashore birdsong. And those sandy scrapes my feet avoided? They're remnants of ancient mountains, long washed into the Atlantic and heaped into isles.

Life's basics abound here. It's the perfect place for people not to build things. In all my time there, the tallest manmade structure on the island belonged to me: my tripod. I was ocean-locked, an astounding turnaround from my youth, on a mission to tell the pelicans' story.

Filming nesting sea turtles demanded that we arrive late and stay late on the island, sometimes to three in the morning. We'd patrol the beach in a battered jeep—dropped there by a helicopter—looking for the telltale scrape marks that betray a female loggerhead turtle's crawl to the dune line.

One night we patrolled until 2:30 in the morning. No turtles. Herbert returned us to the landing in predawn darkness. We moved through the night unseen, like nighthawks. Faint light filled the sky, an accretion from Charleston and its suburbs. It seemed otherworldly.

We came back a week later. We hoped to find a turtle in the process of nesting, a sure thing. A turtle deep into nesting is, in a sense, paralyzed. She will not move once her eggs begin to fall—as poachers know all too well.

We set out around 9 P.M. beneath a full moon. Palmetto fronds splintered the moon-shadowed ground into slivers of white, black, and silver. The marsh grasses and water shone silvery white. We patrolled a snow-white beach beneath luminous stars and a dazzling moon, a beautiful evening for luminaries such as nesting turtles.

Close to midnight, we got out of the jeep again and walked north scanning the milky surf, which rushed in, flirting with our feet, before melting away. Nothing. For a long time the surf fell endlessly upon itself in a wavering line of gleaming water. Then a break, a concentrated area of darkness 30 yards up, interrupted the glowing foam. A log had floated ashore. I nudged it with my foot, and seafaring foxfire, pale green light like the aurora borealis, shimmered down the log's length.

We kept patrolling. Around 3 A.M. we spotted a scrape running up to the dune line. Herbert circled behind the dune line to see how far along the nesting process might be. Soon he ran back, breathless. She was on the nest.

We walked up to a massive dune where a turtle was dropping Ping-Pong-ball-like eggs into a hole. This was no ordinary dune. It was *the* dune. A turtle comes back to lay eggs where she hatched. No one knows how they accomplish this miraculous navigation.

Covered with barnacles and shells, she smelled earthy, organic, hinting of salt and sulfur. Tears oozed from her eyes.

We watched her finish, cover the eggs with her flippers, dig another hole, and cover it to confuse raccoons. Then she crawled into the surf and disappeared beneath the dark, cresting Atlantic. Her babies would incubate in sun-warmed sand, nature's hatchery. Someday the few hatchlings that survived would return and begin the cycle anew.

Cape Romain and its wild islands never failed to give me the feeling I was in the tropics. A sense of mystery and awe gripped me there and it never let go. It was a world I could only dream about as a boy. It inspired me to write a novel. It was unpredictable and dangerous. That slab of mud that just fell off the bank was not mud; it was a bull gator curious to check me out.

I was last at Cape Romain in August 1983. As I stepped into Herbert's Whaler for the last time, a wind ghosting over sun-struck salt marsh kissed me goodbye. I was about to change careers. I wouldn't be back.

Now and then friends tell me they're going to Myrtle Beach. "Can't wait to see the beach," they tell me. And off they go. The real beach, I know, is something they'll never see.

In 2007 I came tantalizingly close to Cape Romain. A friend and I drove down for an oyster roast at a farm overlooking an Awendaw estuary. It was a brisk Saturday early in March. Belted Galloway cattle dotted the pastures. The cows' saddle oxford hides of black and white had everyone's attention, everyone's except mine. I stared at the estuary. Somewhere out there the pelicans would soon begin nesting.

For a few moments I was back. I stood there remembering my days and nights on the islands. I was back where dolphins run in and out of the estuary and loggerhead turtles crawl duneward. There in that sun-blasted, silver-moon islandscape, there in that sea-level garden of sand, sea, and sun, I captured memories as I told a story about a place that's for the birds, a place far from my Georgia home.

·{ FIRE TOWERS AND WINDMILLS }·

As a boy riding in the backseat of Dad's car I looked for two structures that always held my attention. To me both ranked alongside log cabins, old barns, and tenant homes when it came to charm. Both added rustic beauty to the land. Both spoke to humanity's resourcefulness, and yet they were too simple to survive. Thus the land began to lose two icons: fire towers and windmills. You see plenty of cell towers, but you see fewer fire towers and windmills; they're condemned to the past much like log cabins, barns, and tenant homes.

How many times was a drive through the country made more memorable thanks to a windmill or a fire tower, and how sad when I came that way again and saw one or both gone. Oh you can still find a few, but you pretty much have to know where to look. You just don't come up on them like you once did. I hate to see them make that one-way trip to a place called the past, but going they are until they are gone, gone, gone.

Fire towers stood on summits to maximize their view. Towers themselves were 100 feet tall. We boys envied the fellow perched on high and romanticized the forest ranger. The loner atop the tower was the "fire lookout" or "towerman," though "towerwoman" works too, as you'll see. The towerman sat in a "cab" looking for telltale signs of fire. Inside the 8-by-8-foot cab was a swiveling chair, a two-way radio, telephone, binoculars, and maybe a small refrigerator. Of course the crucial equipment was the alidade, a surveying instrument, and a topographic map. In unison, these tools helped the towerman pinpoint a fire's location.

The peak of the fire tower's reign was 1953, when 5,060 towers looked out on the land. Fire towers graced the horizon in abundance as Franklin Roosevelt's Civilian Conservation Corps put young men and World War I veterans to work during the Depression. The CCC built a lot of good things for the country, among them the great and beautiful Blue Ridge Parkway and fire towers where life was lonely at the top.

Shirley Williams knows how lonely it gets. She sat atop a Georgia Forestry Commission fire lookout tower for well over 40 years. The *Savannah Morning News* ran a story on Shirley, who staffed a fire tower down near Ludowici, Georgia. Now, getting paid to sit and look at trees isn't a bad job. Shirley said you could see for 25 miles on a clear day. Beautiful sunsets were the rule, not the exception. "And you haven't lived until you've been in a fire tower during a lightning storm." Otherwise, "up there," she added, "it's quiet and peaceful; not a lot going on." When all seemed quiet, a nap no doubt was possible. Who was around to catch you sleeping on the job? An aspiring writer would have loved being a fire lookout—all those stress-free days and a view that inspires. And then there were moments of intense excitement, a blue curl of smoke on the horizon. Time for action! Perhaps I missed my calling.

I climbed the tower back home just once. Up the steps I went until I reached the trap door. Pushing through, I could see far and wide down Highway 378. Not one for heights, I didn't stay long. I wish now I had. Gazing down across the flatlands is an opportunity you can only poach now, if you've got the courage to climb rickety steps. Of the towers you see few if any are active, and they're not maintained like they once were.

In high school a classmate claimed he took a chicken up the old tower and threw it off. Squawking and spiraling, it made it to the ground. I suspect that chicken made it to the county line in record time. Whenever I see a fire tower I think of that chicken and wonder what in fact happened to it.

Several things brought an end to fire towers' reign—spotters in airplanes and helicopters, satellites, video cameras, cell phones, improvements in radio, and a "let it burn" philosophy for managed forests. Time was that all forest fires were the enemy. Now we know that certain fires are good for the ecosystem. Change marches on and now this romantic symbol of conservation and safety faces hard times. Here and there a few still perform their duty. Satellites detect fires after they are well under way and cell phones in remote areas enjoy no service. Lookouts still climb a few fire towers because having a pair of eyes is still the best option. As for windmills, every time I see one my mind conjures up the Australian outback, famous for its parched landscape. Relics with their face always facing the wind, they touch the land in a lovely way. Acting also as a weathervane, they betray which way the wind blows. Quiet except perhaps for a squeak now and then, windmills work with nature to give us the most reliable, most efficient pumping machine ever invented.

When I take I-20 West to Georgia I always look for a small farm on the right about 35 minutes out of Columbia. As long as I can remember, a windmill has stood there just beyond a small pond. It's standing up pretty well to the winds of change. I have no idea if it gets maintained or if it's just a stubborn survivor. I know that one day it will be gone and that stretch of road will be diminished.

In my travels across Georgia and South Carolina I still come across a few windmills. Up in the foothills I spotted a clapboard outbuilding, a rusty old truck, and what seemed to be an abandoned farm presided over by a stately windmill. It was a welcome scene from the past.

The old windmills we see were built by Aermotor Windmill, a company in San Angelo, Texas. It's hard to believe but it's still in business. My hope for Aermotor is simple. Long may it endure.

Technology is giving us personal windmills. Maybe it'll become fashionable to put a small wind turbine on a nearby hill or in the back yard. Don't expect these modern windmills to display the character of the old windmills. I doubt few schoolchildren will draw a cell tower as we used to draw windmills, blades a-spinning. I like to think that windmills will endure simply because of their "green" nature and primitive beauty, but I'm tilting at the wind. They're goners, just like fire towers.

Down in the lowcountry, lighthouses have long garnered glory for bringing a picturesque touch to the coast. Artists paint them over and over, and photographers love 'em, too. Inland, we had fire towers and windmills, though lighthouses ascended to legend far more than fire towers and windmills ever could. At least lighthouses and cell towers have something in common. When the sun goes down, fire towers and windmills hide in the dark. Not so those blinking cell towers that call attention to themselves.

Come dawn it's a new day. A fire tower standing vigilant over a green forest or a squeaky old windmill spinning a bit wobbly trumps a cell tower any day. Folks will photograph fire towers and windmills as long as they stand, and when it comes to the pecking order of charming structures on the horizon, lighthouses come in first as windmills and fire towers duke it out for second.

Times were, a hex or whammy would do your enemy some good.
The price of a good whammy today is cost-prohibitive,
making voodoo a do-it-yourself project.

PHOTOGRAPH BY THE AUTHOR.

LEGENDS, VOODOO, AND MAYHEM

Georgialina, like most parts of the South, has epic tales and characters. One legend roamed the land in a wagon hitched to goats. "Everybody's a goat; they just don't know it." So proclaimed Ches McCartney, the Goat Man.

In the 1950s, one of Dad's pulpwooders fell ill. "Someone put a root on me, Mr. Junior." Whammy was his name, and he said he couldn't work because a hex had filled his stomach with live lizards. Years later the writing life would take me to the lowcountry, where I'd get serious exposure to that old black magic, voodoo.

A mule kick set a chain of murder into action that killed eight people, reinforcing the South's stature as a place where mayhem can break out when you least expect it, mayhem that involves politicians of the highest order. And once upon a time we had as many covered bridges as Madison County of film lore. One still stands, a glorious relic to a glorious time.

·{ THE GOAT MAN }·

Wherever he went, he caused a stir, and he caused a commotion in Lincoln County as well. He looked like an Old Testament prophet with his long grey beard and tattered clothes. I doubt a more colorful character ever blessed the county with his presence.

His old iron-wheeled wagon hauled a teetering pile of garbage, lanterns, bedding, hay bales, clothes, a potbelly stove, and scrap metal. The big handmade wagon, which clanked and rattled along with car tags from various states adorning its sides, looked like something the Darling family of *The Andy Griffith Show* might commandeer.

He traveled through the county in that rickety old wagon led by goats. An itinerant preacher, he was the legendary Goat Man. He rarely bathed, and you could smell him long before you got close to him. "The goats have taught me a lot in the past 30 years," someone heard Charles "Ches" McCartney say. "They don't, for example, care how I smell or how I look." Goats were his passion. Sick and injured goats got to ride in his wagon. He was fond of saying "Everybody's a goat; they just don't know it."

It was in the early sixties, spring I believe, when he came through Lincoln County. We all piled into the car and headed out to Highway 378, where he had camped out. I remember being a bit uneasy around this bizarre character, his goats, and his outlandish wagon. He was gathering wild onions and greens for a salad. He explained to my mom how he knew which plants to eat and then milked a goat. That was my one Goat Man sighting.

"Ches" McCartney, the Goat Man, wandered the South for four decades. No writer could conjure up such a character. (As Dave Barry says, I am not making any of this up.) It's not surprising that this eccentric vagabond inspired the writers Flannery O'Connor and Cormac McCarthy to base characters on him. Darryl Patton wrote a book about him, *America's Goat Man*, and Duane Branam wrote a song about him, "The Legend."

McCartney's legend began July 6, 1901, in Sigourney, Iowa, though some disagreement attends 1901 as his birth year. At the age of 14, he ran away from his family's farm. He married a Spanish knife thrower ten years his senior in New York and joined her act, serving as her nervous, quaking target. When she became pregnant they decided to farm for a living, but the Great Depression wiped them out. One day just before dawn, his knife-throwing, farming wife vamoosed. McCartney would marry at least two more times.

In 1935, an unbelievable experience changed McCartney's life. He was working for the WPA cutting timber when a tree fell across his body. Several hours elapsed before he was found. Pronounced dead, he was taken to a morgue. Only when the mortician inserted an embalming needle in his arm did he awake. Of the experience McCartney said, "The undertaker was slow and by the time he got around to working on me, the life came back into my body and I regained consciousness. It was as if I had been raised from the dead."

This startling escape from death infused him with religion, and his spiritual awakening inspired him to hitch up the goats and spread the gospel. His wife made goatskin clothes for him to wear but quickly tired of her husband's crusade and left him. (One account claims McCartney sold his wife to another farmer for $1,000.)

McCartney traveled the land with just two books: *Robinson Crusoe*, which inspired his wanderlust, and the Bible. While spreading the Word, he lived off the land, handouts, and his goats. He sold postcards with his image on them for spending money.

Children of the 1960s far and wide remember this folk legend who provoked fear and awe and sadly invited violence. He was mugged more than once, and in one instance the muggers killed two of his beloved goats.

For reasons unknown, this wayfaring minister settled in Twiggs County, Georgia, where he established the Free Thinking Christian Mission. From his mission base, he journeyed out with his goat-drawn wagon to preach his message of eternal damnation for sinners. You could trace his route through the countryside by the wooden signs he nailed to trees, reading "Prepare to Meet Thy God" and illustrated by an image of the fires of Hell burning.

A man of the cloth (he claimed to be ordained), he nonetheless had his foibles. In 1985 McCartney set out for California, hoping to meet the actress Morgan Fairchild, whom he intended to woo and marry. Soon after he arrived in Los Angeles, muggers got him yet again and he had to be hospitalized.

He returned to Georgia and left the road for good in 1987, leaving a legend behind him.

After retiring from the road, McCartney, with his son, Albert Gene, lived in a wooden shack without running water or electricity. When it burned, he and his son moved into a rusted old school bus.

In 1987, he entered a nursing home in Macon, where he lived out his final years as a local celebrity, often wearing a Georgia Bulldog cap. In June 1998 someone shot his son to death in Twiggs County, a murder that remains unsolved. Less than six months after his son's death, the Goat Man died in the Eastview Nursing Home on November 15, 1998. He claimed to be 106. While that may not be true, he led a life the likes of which we'll never see again. There's no disputing that.

The Goat Man was something to behold. Seeing him rattling down the road was as iconic as seeing "See Rock City" atop a barn's roof. He was a roadside attraction like no other, compelling people to get out of their cars and gawk. Old-timers say it was way too easy spotting experienced Goat Man observers in a big crowd. They were the ones standing upwind.

·{ BLACK MAGIC }·

That old black magic has long been a part of Southern culture. Back in the 1950s Dad ran a small pulpwood business. One of his workers would fall ill now and then. He often told Dad, "Someone put a root on me." One time he couldn't work, he said, because his "stomach was full of live lizards," and he was absolutely convinced someone had put a root on him. The fellow's name was even a term for a hex, Whammy.

Now this black magic, voodoo, hoodoo, or whatever you choose to call it is nothing to dismiss. It has a long history, and it has, indeed, killed people. The key to its morbid success is faith. If victims truly believe they're under a spell, then for all practical purposes they are.

As for dying from black magic, that happens when a root doctor gives a "patient" medicine that inadvertently poisons him. Voodoo has long presented law enforcement with a big headache.

Down in the South Carolina lowcountry, the late high sheriff of Beaufort County, Ed McTeer, made a name for himself as a root doctor. I met the good sheriff in 1978, and he was full of tales. Here is but one.

A witch doctor put a "blue root" on an old black woman, and death was knocking on her door. McTeer, a white sheriff, had studied root medicine so that he could better deal with its practitioners and their spells for a practical reason: he routinely encountered both. To better enforce the law, he realized he had to master black magic. He did, and his reputation spread.

McTeer arrived at the woman's house. He then donned his blue sunglasses, a sure sign he was a root doctor. "I know that there is evil working in this place," he said. "I can feel it in my bones."

McTeer told the small crowd gathered around the ill woman that he would cure her. He then went into a trance, wildly circling the yard while mumbling incantations. Suddenly, the woman sat up. As she did, McTeer bayed like a wild dog and jumped over to her steps, where he yanked the offending root out and waved it over his head for all to see.

The crowd shrank back in fright but turned jubilant when McTeer tossed the evil root into the nearby estuary. McTeer had planted the root to guarantee that his conjuring would be a smash hit.

A week later McTeer paid the woman a visit. She was back to her old self. But what if McTeer had not intervened? Most likely she would have wasted away and died.

One day near Edisto Island I was driving a stretch of highway that well could have been a lowcountry postcard. The road shot through a tunnel of live oaks heavy with Spanish moss. Rounding a curve, I came across a shanty painted sky blue (think Tar Heel blue) to ward off evil spirits. Some folks refer to it as "haint blue," because an evil spirit can't pass through that color.

As I drove past the house a small bridge appeared ahead. To its right stood a dead tree with amulets and blue bottles hanging from its limbs.

It's a wicked thing, this voodoo. Down in New Orleans I walked into a voodoo shop on Bourbon Street. A strange place, this shop, with its voodoo dolls and amulets suspended from the walls and ceilings. A strange incense filled the air, hazy, aromatic, yet threatening.

I found a book, *Voodoo & Hoodoo*, and took it to the sales clerk. Suddenly, the proprietor, a dark-haired woman, appeared from nowhere, making a scene.

"Are you going to kill someone with this book?" she demanded.

"No, just researching the subject," I replied. People filled her cramped shop, and they turned toward me as if they were about to see what a real murderer looks like.

On page 115, I found an ominous section, "To Kill Someone." Right off, the book states, "not much killing is done anymore. It is just too expensive—up to $500 in good times." Now understand that this book carries a 1978 copyright, so adjusting for inflation and factoring in today's bad economy, I'd say the cost for a fatal whammy today ought to run about $900. So is voodoo a DIY deal? Here are three ways to put a fatal hex on someone.

Nail Him—Take a photograph of the intended victim and nail it face-side down against the north side of a tree. For the next nine mornings drive a nail into the photograph. The victim will become progressively weaker and die on the ninth day.

A Lock—Get a lock of the intended victim's hair as well as his or her photograph. Bury the two together, preferably in mud or a moist area where the objects will disintegrate quickly. As they disintegrate, so will the victim.

Sock It to Him—Get a sock or stocking belonging to the intended victim. Put graveyard dirt in it and bury it under the victim's front steps. In three weeks the victim will be dead, having mysteriously withered away.

Got any enemies? You're not missing a sock or stocking, are you? Where do you get your hair cut? Getting a lock would be easy. Having mysterious problems around your home? Put up a bottle tree. Nothing like some blue bottles to cure black magic. Bottle trees are as Southern as can be, and I see them all the time, leading me to wonder if people just think they're pretty or if they know their real purpose.

A beautiful blue bottle, deep blue like indigo, will lure a spirit of the night inside, and come morning sunlight will destroy it. Some say the wind cooing past a bottle tempts spirits to enter it, whereupon they are trapped.

Blue bottles, if you believe, may cure your evil spirits problem. Whether you believe or not, if you put one up you'll help preserve a Southern tradition. As to whether bottles capture evil spirits, well, the answer is blowing in the wind.

.⸙ HOW A MULE KICK KILLED ⸙. EIGHT PEOPLE

You can drive by a place 1,000 times and be unaware of its history. Such was the case for a small country store on Highway 378 in Edgefield County. Over the years I've passed the little store 1,000 times and not once did I stop. That changed Sunday, October 13. I did pass it, but I turned around and went back, curious to see what the price of gas was on the old rusty pump.

I got out with my camera, and a classic RC Cola sign immediately distracted me. Behind it was another vintage sign advertising Camel cigarettes. American Pickers would like this place I thought. I moved closer to get a good shot. That's when a man slipped up behind me.

"If you think I'm selling those signs you're wrong."

Startled, I said, "No, I just wanted to photograph the old gas pump and the signs caught my attention."

"People try to buy them all the time."

"It's a wonder someone hasn't stolen them," I replied.

"Maybe I'll file off the nail heads," he said, and then he paused. "My granddad got killed in that store."

"Robbed and shot?"

"No, a woman had him killed for $500."

And then the most incredible story unfolded, a story that goes back to 1941. The little store at the intersection of Highway 378 and

Highway 430, a road that leads to Edgefield, a road known as Meeting Street, holds deep, dark secrets.

In 1941 roads were unpaved and in many areas electrification had yet to arrive. Men farmed with mules. Times were tough; people were rough. It must have been an upsetting thing to lose a calf. Yes, to lose a calf was to lose an investment. When a mule wandered from one Edgefield County farm onto an adjacent farm and kicked a calf, killing it, someone had to pay for it.

That someone was the granddad of the fellow standing beside me. "Yep, my granddad was shot in the back for $500. Right in there," he said, pointing at the store's old wooden siding.

Murderpedia, an online encyclopedia devoted to those who kill other people, documents this tale of dead livestock and lives gone wrong. It quotes a report that appeared at EdgefieldDaily.com, which I provide here as the facts have been vetted.

> The story began in September of 1940 when Davis Timmerman's mule got into Wallace Logue's field and the mule kicked and killed Logue's calf. Logue demanded that Timmerman pay him $20 for the calf and Timmerman agreed. Logue later went to Timmerman's rural store and decided he wanted $40 in restitution instead of $20 and Timmerman refused to pay.
>
> Logue became infuriated, grabbed an ax handle, and began beating Timmerman. Timmerman pulled a gun he kept hidden in a drawer, shot twice, and killed Logue. Timmerman was said to have locked the body in store and, despite being seriously injured, drove to Edgefield to report the shooting to then Sheriff L.H. Harling.
>
> Sheriff Harling, Coroner John Hollingsworth, and Solicitor Jeff Griffith drove back to the store. Based on their interpretation of the evidence, Timmerman was held over for trial. After the trial the jury ruled Timmerman acted in self-defense and he was acquitted.
>
> Logue's widow, Sue, and his brother, George, didn't agree with the jury's verdict. They hired Joe Frank Logue, George

and Wallace's nephew, giving him $500 to find somebody to kill Timmerman. Joe Frank was an officer with the Spartanburg Police Department and he hired Clarence Bagwell to do the job.

A year after Wallace died, Joe Frank and Bagwell went to Timmerman's store. Joe Frank waited in the car while Bagwell went in and asked for a pack of cigarettes (some say it was a pack of gum). When Timmerman turned to get the item Bagwell fired five shots at point-blank range with a .38 caliber revolver, killing him instantly.

Joe Frank and Bagwell returned back to Spartanburg and carried on as if nothing happened. Unfortunately for the pair, Bagwell was a heavy drinker and during one of his binges bragged to a young woman that he had made $500 for killing a man.

The woman went to police. When Bagwell was questioned, he learned that he had been seen at Timmerman's store on the day of the murder. Other reports say he was spotted casing the store prior to the murder as well. Either way, feeling trapped, Bagwell confessed and fingered Joe Frank as well.

It turned out Joe Frank wasn't a dutiful nephew after all. He admitted hiring Bagwell, and also told the authorities that the money had come from his aunt and uncle, Sue and George Logue.

On Sunday, Nov. 16, 1941, newly elected Sheriff Wad Allen and Deputy W.L. "Doc" Clark picked up the warrants from magistrate A.L. Kemp and headed for Sue Logue's home.

But someone had warned George Logue that the law was on the way. Logue and a sharecropper, Fred Dorn, ambushed the two officers. Sheriff Allen died after being shot in the head and Deputy Clark was shot in the stomach and arm. Clark was able to wound both men before staggering from the house and making his way to Highway 378 where he was picked up by a passing motorist.

Gov. R.M. Jeffries later ordered state patrolmen and deputies from Saluda County to arrest Logue and Dorn.

With dozens of officers surrounding the house, and officials wanting to avert further bloodshed, they appealed to then local Circuit Court Judge Strom Thurmond, a Logue family friend, to try to reason with the Logues. Thurmond walked alone across the yard and into the house. The Logues followed his advice and surrendered a short time later.

Two days later, Deputy Clark died. Logue's friend, Fred Dorn, died the day before.

Four months later, George, Sue, and Bagwell were tried for Timmerman's murder. The three-day trial was held in Lexington County with Solicitor Griffith serving as prosecutor.

The jury took only two hours to convict the trio.

On Jan. 15, 1943, Sue Logue was electrocuted. One book reports that Strom Thurmond accompanied Sue on the trip to the "death house" and had relations with her during the trip, according to Thurmond's driver interviewed for the book. (She had been a teacher in the school system when Strom was superintendent. A tale goes that Sue and Strom were caught in the act, in flagrante delicto.)

Sue Logue was the first and only woman to die in the electric chair in South Carolina.

Less than an hour after Sue was executed, George and Bagwell took their place in the electric chair.

Joe Frank Logue received the death penalty for his participation in the killing and his execution date was set for Jan. 23, 1944. He ate his last meal and was prepped for the electric chair. Shortly before midnight, Gov. Olin D. Johnston visited Joe Frank and as a result of that visit, Johnston commuted Joe Frank Logue's sentence to life.

(Courtesy of Roy Blackwell, editor, *Edgefield Daily*, EdgefieldDaily.com)

I'll never pass that way again that I don't think of the murders and Sue Logue. On the evening before her execution, she cried softly as her long black hair was shaved off.

Oh! I almost forgot. The price of gas on the old pump was sixty cents a gallon. That pump must have last dispensed gas circa 1974, about the time I first passed this store where a mule's kick set a series of tragedies in motion.

·{ TENANT HOMES }·

A trip down a secondary road through farm country used to turn up elegant little houses resting on rock piles. They stood alone, sentinels looking over fields. Now they are rare. Referred to as saltbox houses, catslides, and pole cabins, they long stood with grace and character in pastures and fields. In their heyday, a sea of white cotton surrounded tenant homes in summer, but as tractors relegated mules, plows, and hoes to obsolescence the homes were abandoned. Today, nothing makes its home in them but wasps, mice, and birds. Weather, vandalism, and sheer neglect have long been destroying them, and few remain. All that's left of many are chimneys and fieldstones.

For generations, plain folk in the South lived in such homes. Many sprang up during Reconstruction, an era of upheaval when being a tenant farmer meant a step up the social ladder. Sharecroppers exchanged a crop for a house and a share of the yield. Still, a tenant farmer often had nothing to show for his efforts at year's end. Many writers portrayed life in the little homes as unbearable. Rita Turner Wall, author of *The Vanishing Tenant Homes of Rural Georgia*, wrote: "life in the old houses was what the occupants made of it: a vegetable garden and a flock of chickens or hard fare, a yard full of flower beds or blank emptiness, a tablecloth or bare boards, a good life or a bad life."

Tenant homes had no plumbing, no built-in sinks, no cabinets, no closets. Generally, only functional furniture such as pie safes, beds, and chairs graced these old homes. Jars and simple containers on crude shelves held the staples. Kerosene lamps broke the darkness. Buckets hauled water up from wells.

Wall wrote that "there is in the pitch of the roof, the shape of chimney, the whole mass, an orderly disposition pleasing to the eye." She's right. I see more beauty in a weathered tenant home than in some sparkling vinyl-sided house. No wonder so many artists and photographers find them fascinating.

Farming changed, jobs went north, and after decades of painting them, patching them, and stuffing newspaper in cracks in the walls, people left tenant homes alone, and that sealed their fate. Few are left to tell their story, but two, it so happens, remain.

I wrote about tenant homes for the newspaper back home in Georgia. Murray Norman read my column and found one he could relocate to the hometown history village. Part of the home's story, we discovered, was told in "The Miracle of a Friendship," an autobiography written by James Robert Colvin, known as J.R.

"A young black man came to work for my Daddy in 1930. John was probably 18 or 19 at that time."

John Bennett was the only person who lived in the little tenant home built by J.R.'s dad. Inside, shelves once stored John Bennett's glasses and dishes, pots and pans. A table with two chairs and a bed were there, too. J.R. wrote, "John kept his house spotlessly clean. His yards were well kept, and he usually had blooming flowers and shrubbery he would obtain from his mother. He and I would go fishing together, go hunting together or would sit by his fireplace during cold, rainy days and play checkers by the hours. . . . We loved and respected each other as if we were brothers." The spark of friendship burned as warm and as strong as the oak logs had in the shack's tiny fireplace so many, many years ago.

I wrote two other homes' story in spring 1986. One home, a catslide—so named because not even a tree-climbing cat could hang onto its steep roof—had a framed Jesus hanging on its wall. A frazzled toothbrush hung from a rusty nail. A survivor, this home had occupants who had tried to modernize it with a sink propped on wooden legs. A miracle called electricity once served the old home's two switches and hanging sockets, but the antiquated meter from the B&C Kearney Company of Tucker, Georgia, clung uselessly to worn clapboard siding. Another effort to modernize the home brings to mind the old adage "they don't make 'em like they used to."

Despite such modernization, the house nonetheless retained its original character. Someone took down one of the original interior doors, an abused but still-beautiful slab of solid wood. In its place stood a contemporary door made from glued fibers set to a frame. The old door, as solid as ever, stood in an unprotected corner beneath an open roof while the modern door, though sheltered from the elements, disintegrated.

Several miles west another tenant home stood with two doors, a duplex. Out back in a creeping line of pines an outhouse waited in vain for a visit from the old house's tenant, but she had died. In fact, the home appeared as if its owner, an elderly lady, just walked away, leaving her modest belongings behind. Her efforts to beautify the place remained. On the mantle stood a Japanese lantern of sorts fashioned from green and yellow foam egg cartons connected by needlepoint thread. Within the lantern's circular bottom an aluminum pie plate held a stub of a candle. On a dark cold night a bit of colored light had brightened this lady's last nights.

Eighteen years after visiting these homes, I went back to see if they were still standing. The catslide was gone. Not even Jesus could save it. Not a trace remained. As for the duplex tenant, if it stood, it hid behind pines. I parked and got out. The home was there, falling in on itself amid a thick grove of malnourished pines. I later learned that the old lady living in it had made soap from lard neighbors had brought her. That explained the lye I had seen.

Textile mills' seductive call of prosperity doomed tenant homes. Wasps, mice, and birds next called them home. Many little shacks found a reprieve for a bit as storage sites for hay, feed, and seed. In nearly every such case, the chimney hangs from the ceiling with its hearth knocked out. That way more hay, what have you, could be stuffed inside.

Ill maintained, if at all, these noble survivors, some 130 years old, first see their roof go. Then the walls sooner or later collapse. The structure crumbles into the earth or is razed. Hard to believe that happens over and over, but it does. Some folks see tenant homes as a blight on the landscape. Damn hard to fathom that. For many years I knew just when to look across a pasture driving down U.S. Highway 78 in Wilkes County, Georgia. What a handsome tenant home stood there. From the road it looked perfect.

Then one fall it was gone. Knocked down. I still look for it every time I pass through and feel a twinge of remorse. As for the few tenant homes still standing, when they cave in and decay, their sad-sweet history will seep into the earth, forever absorbed. Gone. At least one is preserved in a history village. It provides us one last glimpse of a culture that long ago succumbed to hard times, but at least we know a bit of its story.

·{ COUNTRY STORES }·

For decades country stores stood as compact centers of commerce ready to dispense most anything and to provide gathering places to socialize. In rural areas, they stood as beacons to anyone who needed a plug of tobacco, a mule collar, most anything, but especially a chance to talk.

A trip to a country store was one of childhood's joys, a time for joyful self-indulgence, sweets, treats, and adventure. My grandfather ran a country store on Georgia Highway 79. He sold minnows from an outside tank. Inside, half-gallon jars with red lids held assorted cookies as big as your hand. The countertops glittered with colorful candies.

He sold penny candies like Mary Janes, those chewy bite-size peanut butter and molasses candies; Lifesavers (the summer candy that withstood heat better than chocolate); and Bazooka Joe bubblegum, staples we loved. Coke with peanuts was great, too. Pour the peanuts into the bottle and enjoy! RC Colas and Moon pies, too.

Granddad sold Beechnut chewing gum and coconut candy with stripes of pink, white, and chocolate flavors. He didn't use a cash register. A wood drawer stored folding money pressed in place by a vintage Ford chrome greyhound hood ornament. It's hard to imagine anyone today keeping hard-earned money in such a simple place, but it was commonplace back then.

A place of commerce, yes, but it was more. It provided a focal point for the community. Mom remembers that Saturday evenings, Bud Sow, a local man, would come and tell animal stories to the children, generally reversing the animals' names. A grasshopper became a hoppergrass. He was a local Uncle Remus of sorts, and the children loved him and his tales.

Men would come and shoot bottle caps at cracks in the floor to see who would end up buying "dopes," an old reference to Coca-Cola, which once contained cocaine. (In its early days, Coca-Cola contained nine milligrams of cocaine per glass.)

Mom recalls as well that her dad's store had a "cat hole" in the floor where a cat came and went. The cat hole proved handy to Mom's sister, Evelyn, for tossing goodies for retrieval later. On one occasion, Evelyn had some fun with her younger brother, Carroll, who was bugging her for some Lifesavers. Superlax, a laxative, looked much like Lifesavers, and she gave him all he wanted. Uncle Carroll spent the rest of the day at the outhouse.

Mom also remembers that Thursday nights, mullet came in on ice from the coast for a fish fry. A country store provided a rhythm of life as well.

I remember my granddad's store and Price's Store, a larger establishment. Crates of drinks were stacked high. Simple bulbs hung from the ceiling. Old men sat on the benches that flanked the front door and shared farming advice over smokes and Cokes.

The coolers at Price's and Granddad's stores were filled with water and ice. You'd fish around getting a Coke from the bottom, pulling it out with a numb hand. First thing you did was check the drink's bottom to see where the magic beverage was bottled.

The coldest Coca-Cola I ever drank came from Price's Store. It was a blazing hot summer day, and I was helping gather hay on my grandfather's farm. Aunt Vivian went to Price's Store and returned with a cooler of Coca-Colas for all the workers. Sitting beneath a persimmon tree, a breeze in my face, I downed my Coke in seconds. So cold it burned.

Country stores sold other drinks. Orange Crush was one. *Rush! Rush! For Orange Crush* was an ad I recall. And then there were the Nehi beverages. Some of you will recall Nehi grape and Nehi orange drinks. (Nehi became Royal Crown Cola in 1955.)

You could buy Nutty Buddy ice cream, BB Bats, candy cigarettes, and Sugar Daddys at a country store. A Sugar Daddy had to be a dentist's best friend because it would just about pull your teeth out. And some of you'll recall Dreamsicles, an orange sherbet ice cream on a stick.

I tip my hat to Cracker Barrel and Mast General. They give to-day's kids the look and feel of a country store . . . old signs and a classic Coca-Cola icebox filled with ice-chilled Cokes. You can still find vintage stores if you look for them. Drive Highway 378 from Lexington into Georgia up through Wilkes County. Better hurry, though. Every time I travel that road, I see where a store has burned and in one case collapsed. They keep surrendering to the elements.

Drive South Carolina "200" roads and you'll come across some of these fine stores. One sultry afternoon I drove Highway 283, a road that suggests the South of the 1950s. I had never been down this backroad, and seeing the old farms and homes along its route put me in a pleasant state. And then not far out of Plum Branch I came across Deerfeathers Store. What a colorful place. The columns holding up the tin overhang are cedar trees painted white. Stubs where limbs were cut no doubt proved convenient for hanging stuff. Croaker sacks come to mind. Beneath the overhang were two homemade benches and an old cable spool, a table of sorts. One concession to modern times, a Pepsi machine, with its bright blue, red, and white branding, appeared out of place against an old cement wall. Grass edging the old store's front seemed undisturbed . . . few feet if any had trod it. It appeared the store hadn't opened in a while, but that's because it opens only for deer and turkey season.

You can be sure men have long chewed the fat here. No doubt they talked 'bout hunting whitetail deer, buck scrapes, and guns. A sign over the door proclaims a tournament: "Deerfeathers 13th Annual Big Buck & Doe Contest." The 14th annual Big Buck and Doe contest took place, but the sign hasn't been updated. Burl Ricker owns the store, and it is the third country store on the site in a span covering more than 100 years. The first two stores burned. The original store, said Ricker, was a two-story affair with a ramp where wagons could load and offload wares. "Highway 283 used to be a dirt road," he said. Imagining dusty old wagons rolling up to the store is easy.

The store onsite has been open for 50 years. The regular gas pump—the only pump—registers gas at $1.86 a gallon. Ricker said he used to sell penny candy, "but they went up on the price." He added that he does have an antique bubble gum dispenser in the store and that I "ought to stop by in April when they are open." I plan to do just that. Oh, one more thing. The name Deerfeathers? It's not some reference to some mutant deer. "My kids picked it out," said Ricker.

Other Deerfeathers are out there. The next time you pass a country store, one that's long closed, its paint peeling, weeds and trees overtaking it, roof sagging, let your imagination loose. Envision it in the prime of life. You're bound to see vintage pick-ups, men in coveralls and ladies in floral print dresses buying provisions and sharing news. You'll see a bench with old men whittling away the day and old glass-bubble gas pumps with gas selling for just a few cents a gallon.

Out back, some boys, no doubt, will be up to no good. You'll find candies, supplies, a freezing Coke, and, best of all, friends inside the vintage country store, yet another victim of that wonderful thing called progress.

·⁌ COVERED BRIDGES ⁋·

I remember, as I grew up, hearing people talk about covered bridges and how pretty they were, but I never saw one and I wasn't sure what they meant by a covered bridge. A bridge with a tarp over it? That didn't sound pretty. The closest thing to a covered bridge I'd seen back then was the Homer Legg Bridge crossing into Columbia County and its latticework of steel. That, to me, qualified as a covered bridge . . . or so I thought.

As an adult I continued to hear about covered bridges but never saw an authentic one until Clint Eastwood directed and starred with Meryl Streep in *The Bridges of Madison County*. That was on the silver screen, though, and my qualification for membership in the "I've Seen a Real Covered Bridge Club" remained on hold.

The years bring knowledge, and now I know that the history of the covered bridge is fairly straightforward. Early bridges in this country were not much more than logs stretched across timbers over creeks. Rudimentary but effective. As bridge building evolved, builders created longer spans, using trusses, arches, and joined stringers. Like most structures early in this country's history, bridges were made almost entirely of wood. And that's where problems developed. The joints of a wooden truss bridge would rot if exposed to the weather. Covering the bridge with a roof solved that problem, and that blessed our culture with a picturesque edifice: the covered bridge.

Today, authentic covered bridges in these parts are as rare as the proverbial hen's teeth. I've seen the covered bridge in Evans at the Woodbridge Subdivision. Apparently it's the creation of a developer who wanted to give his community a unique identity, and he did.

Up in Oconee County you can find a quaint span from the old days that's been restored. The bridge goes over Red Oak Creek and was built in 1840. It's not open for traffic, and that's a good thing. As you'd expect, a historical marker tells passersby about the old bridge.

According to the Georgia Covered Bridges List, compiled in October 2009, Lincoln County has a covered bridge. Privately owned and built in 1994, it's 41 feet long. It's not, obviously, one of the old bridges.

Back in February 2007 I came across the real deal: a covered bridge up in northern Greenville, South Carolina. I was up for the production of *Leatherheads* and had some time to kill one afternoon. I was riding around checking out the countryside. It was late afternoon, when sunlight comes in so low everything is gold and lustrous despite the blue winter light, but driving is hard. A bit blinded as I rounded a curve, I got quite a shock as my eyes adjusted. I saw a bridge I'd seen on a daily basis! It's the bridge in a Robert Clark photograph, framed and hanging in my house, Campbell's Covered Bridge. Suddenly, without warning, I was a member of the "I've Seen a Real Covered Bridge Club." This covered bridge sits near the small town of Gowensville. It's South Carolina's last remaining covered bridge, and it crosses Beaverdam Creek. Greenville County owns the bridge and closed it to traffic in the early 1980s. It was added to the National Register of Historic Places on July 1, 2009.

I got out and walked onto the old bridge, struck by its narrow width. Beneath the wooden flooring, Beaverdam Creek ran cold and swift over rocks. Everything was peaceful, the air a bit chilled. I stayed there a while trying to envision a time many years before when traffic rolled through and no one gave a second thought to the bridge's uniqueness. It would have made for a nice spot for couples, once the busy day settled down. I walked out from the bridge as darkness settled in, and sure enough, a young couple drove up. They looked at me, a stranger, as if I didn't belong there, and I didn't. I was glad to see the old bridge still had allure, still had its pull on romantic souls.

A dirt road, a church, an oak tree, and an old barn compose a classic scene of the old South. All that's needed is a cinder-sparking locomotive. Could that be one materializing from the fog?

❦ SENTIMENTAL JOURNEY ❦

For many of us a certain summer lives with us the rest of our life; we can't shake what it meant. It marked a transition of sorts, and for many there's that one job that stands out. It wasn't about money. It was about the phase we were in and the people it brought into our life. Through changing times we amass a personal history that can be heartwarming, diverting, and bittersweet but unforgettable.

The times they do change. Places come and go, jobs come and go, and memorable people vanish. Old black gentlemen, a colonel who turned to growing camellias, travel by bus and train, and the ways of American Indians remain as colorful as ever, though not as common. We never forget, though. All it takes is one word, one reminder, and we recall who we used to be, where we came from, and who we became. We marvel too at the lives of others.

THE SUMMER OF 1967

Something about summer burns its way into our memory, and it's not the summer sun. Summer just seems to be a time for taking account of things. Remembering special moments, friends, those no longer with us, and crystallizing events when memory turned photographic. Times when you still see the past as clearly as a crackling yellow-blue lightning bolt. For me, and for you, too, I bet, there's that one summer you keep going back to.

We all have a summer that stands out from the rest if we think about it. The other day I asked a friend if any of her summers were special. She was quick to say, "No." She paused and a shadow crossed her face. "Yes," she said, "the day Daddy told us he was leaving and never coming back." And he didn't.

I spend a lot of time looking backwards. Maybe you do, too. I think a lot about the people I knew back then more so than those I know today. Sometimes life really does seem like a journey . . . we're all just passing through. Friends come and go . . . places come and go . . . the only constant is self. Maybe you feel that way, too. In the journey that has been my life I keep going back to the one summer that stands out above the rest: the summer of 1967.

It was my last summer of being free and irresponsible. I had graduated from high school, and college was four months away. It was, in a real way, my last summer to be what I had always been, a nobody, but you can't be a nobody all your life.

College and a whole new world awaited me that fall. I worked that summer in Washington, Georgia, at the Almar Rainwear plant. I carpooled to the plant with Dawkins Holloway, a fellow high school graduate. We worked in shipping, packing boxes of bright yellow plastic rain suits destined for points I can't recall. The suits, heat-sealed together, I do remember, would come apart as soon as you put them on. We stole a few.

My plans to room at Georgia with Dawkins that autumn fell apart, too. He married Peggy Culbertson, and that sent me to college with random roommates my freshman year, a year that should have been fun but wasn't.

That summer stands out for other reasons. People were talking a lot about a place called Vietnam. A friend I played football with, Stanley Scott, had been killed on August 12. The war seemed far away until Stanley died. We had to wait all summer for his funeral. I remember the mournful trumpet solo at his service. And then a member of my church, Benny Myers, got shot up in 'Nam, a burst from a machine gun. He was never the same and died after falling from a tree stand while deer hunting.

I had been accepted at the University of Georgia, but the truth is I felt anything but safe. The war seemed closer than ever, and the new life awaiting me was one big question mark. I felt a sort of dread that summer, a sort of emotional seasickness or homesickness. Leaving home for a long time was something I wasn't good at. I'd never done it. I could not describe the feeling I harbored that summer, but it was there, a troubling presence that never took leave.

And then late one afternoon, Mike Bentley, Dawkins Holloway, Charles Lewis (we called him "Zewis"), and I were down at the lake at a little side road opposite Elijah Clark State Park listening to a radio blaring from a car with wide-open doors. Across the water was South Carolina, a place I knew little about except that you could buy a beer over there and nobody cared. We skipped rocks across the water.

As we looked for flat rocks and talked much about nothing, a song came over the radio, a haunting dirge-like melody that captured the isolation, uncertainty, and fear within me. From the first mournful note of Procul Harum's "A Whiter Shade of Pale," Mike, Dawkins, Charles, and I were summoned: we walked toward the radio.

The melancholy music and the mysterious lyrics mesmerize me to this day. To this day the requiem-like lyrics and the Hammond 102 organ's haunting notes dredge up that afternoon by the lake. The song was, in a way, prophetic. One interpretation of "a whiter shade of pale" is that it refers to death, literally turning whiter like a corpse.

Dawkins is gone. Car wreck. Mike is gone. Heart attack. Charles is gone. Car wreck. I alone would escape. I alone hold onto that afternoon by the lake. The dice roll and some lose. Life goes on.

The summer of 1967 would be known as the summer of love, but that didn't apply to me. I didn't know anything about hippies, flower power, and hashish, and I didn't protest anything. I just think of that summer as my last spurt of youthful abandon. After it, life was never the same.

Life wouldn't change dramatically, but a series of small changes and new directions, step by step by misstep, accumulated and in the long run made for dramatic change. Marriage. Children. Divorce. . . .

Music surely made that summer memorable. Earlier in June, just a few days after I had graduated from high school, a moment occurred that lives in me still. Like a surreal scene from an old movie, sepia-toned with splashes of color here and there, a wavering scratch line running its length, that afternoon plays in my mind. I was working on my first car, a 1961 Corvair, a white four-door car that ran some days and some days didn't. On this day it didn't. Hearing a car slow down on the Augusta Highway, I turned from the rear-engine compartment, and down the driveway came two angels: Cheryl Stewart and Margaret Harper, two of the most beautiful girls I remember from youth. Dashing from the car, Cheryl held an album; Margaret shouted, "You have got to hear this now."

The album they held would change everything. We played it all afternoon. The British Invasion had turned American music on its ear, but *Sergeant Pepper's Lonely Hearts Club Band* was about to change the world. The Beatles, weary of live performances, had abandoned the stage for the studio, and this masterpiece, the brainchild of Paul McCartney and produced by George Martin, came out of the Abbey Road Studios to storm the world.

Clothes, value shifts, hairstyles, the way albums would be recorded, the drug culture, protests—all of that burst across the sky when *Sergeant Pepper* hit the airways. Mom remarked that just when I was to go to college and look my best in preppy clothes, the era of long hair, bell bottoms, and tie-dyed T-shirts took over. Suddenly, you didn't wear shoes; you wore sandals made from truck tires. But you can't wear stuff like that forever. Thus began for me that summer a long road of searching for an identity.

For me and for many others, music, the loss of innocence, and pivotal life changes all came together that summer. I was forced to adapt to people I had not grown up with, people who had always been and would always be different from me.

In life we come across times we just can't forget; we can't exactly say why those times matter, but they do. Deep inside, we sense that we took a step in a new direction, that of becoming who we would ultimately be. For me, it was the summer of 1967. War, death, music, girls, the loss of friends, self-identity, and more bubbled and boiled in a broth where the person I was to be was cooking up. It just took a lot of time to make sense of it all.

I'm sure you can point to one summer as more memorable, more meaningful than any other. Where were you when that one unforgettable summer put its stamp on you? And what did it make of you?

·{ THE SAD BALLAD OF MOSES CORLEY }·

We all cross paths with a person we can't forget. It can be a chance encounter or a day-to-day type thing. And that person doesn't have to be a celebrity, wealthy, or powerful. A simple man can stay with you all your life. And so a man by the beautiful name of Moses Corley lingers in my mind. If every life is a song, then Moses's life was a sad, sad ballad.

Moses was old school, you could say. An Uncle Tom, others might add. He worked as the janitor in the library of a small church-supported college where I once taught. He loved his job. Said it was the best job he ever had. Hoped to retire there.

He always referred to me as "Mr. Tom" and peppered his speech with "Yes, sirs" and "No, sirs." It was a habit I couldn't get him to break. It was ingrained, a way of life. He'd laugh at my jokes and slap his knees and his infectious laugh was unforgettable. That was long ago . . . 1977.

Even now I can see him sweeping the lab in the library basement where I taught. His snow-white Afro was stately, and a cataract gave him an owlish gaze. His left eye, white as milk glass, stared into space. When he looked at you, he was there and yet he wasn't. But he was memorable for his sweet nature, a prince of a man. He had a wife with diabetes, and he talked about her constantly. He doted on her. She was his sun, moon, and stars. She was bedridden, had lost a leg, and her chief joy in life was watching TV.

Back then I taught Education 155, Audio-Visual Methods, for aspiring elementary education teachers. The days of the computer were light-years away, and the technology was embarrassingly simple. One method I taught was how to make colored overhead transparencies. Like I said, embarrassingly simple. My students use colored acetate to give their transparencies impact. They'd cut out shapes, and the acetate would cling to the transparency thanks to static electricity. At the end of the day, colored scraps of acetate littered the carpeted floor like some image from a kaleidoscope knocked askew. It was a mess, but a colorful mess.

One day just before the Christmas break a few students were working late when Moses came in to clean the lab. I noticed how closely he watched one student work on a food group presentation: red apples, yellow bananas, oranges, and so forth. She'd cut the shapes out and stick them onto the clear transparency. He watched her position the acetate, and after a while he began to clean up the scraps.

Each day, Moses had done just that: clean up the scraps and trash them. So when I noticed Moses was picking up scraps of acetate and carefully placing them in a box, I was curious.

"Moses," I said, "what are you going to do with those?"

"Mr. Tom, my wife's got one leg and has the diabetes. All she can do is lie in bed and watch TV. I promised her I'd give her a color TV some day. I'm gonna make her one for Christmas. I'll take these home and stick 'em on the TV and she can see in color!" The excitement in his voice was something. He'd figured a way to overcome a problem. Making good on a promise to his beloved wife. A special Christmas gift. It was such a sweet thing. It touched me.

Not long after that, Moses asked me a favor. Could he borrow $10?

"Sure," I said, and handed him a ten. He asked other faculty members, too, but one ratted him out. A new janitor took his place. He'd been fired. A few months later I got my first writing position and left the college and began working downtown. I assumed Moses was working somewhere else, too. I tried to find him but had no luck. He stayed with me though. I couldn't forget him.

A few years went by. One cold, windy November day I ventured out for lunch at a small Italian restaurant. As I walked past the bus station, I saw a pair of legs sticking out of a green dumpster just beyond a dieseling Greyhound. Out popped Moses Corley, bedraggled, and in need of a haircut. Seeing him was a joy, tempered by the obvious fact that he was in dire straits.

"Moses," I shouted, "it's me, Tom!"

Slowly he walked over. He couldn't look me in the eye. After some embarrassment, he began to talk. He had lost his home, and his wife had died. That infectious laugh had died, too. His spirit was broken. I gave him $20 and offered some useless advice on jobs. We talked a bit and parted ways. He had no phone, no address, a refugee exiled to the streets because he had asked the wrong person for a lousy $10. I never saw him again.

I drove past a group of homeless people once, a self-important woman alongside for the ride. "You'd think those men would get a job," she said. "Any job." In a way she was right, but I knew too that for some there is that high-water mark. That job that is the best you'll ever have and if you lose it . . . well, life can sure go downhill.

I know other Moses Corleys are out there, homeless, hungry, and heartbroken. I'm sure the Moses I knew left this green earth long ago to join his wife. And I know they are together again, up there, watching the biggest, most colorful flat-screen TV ever imagined. It's warm, food's on the table, and there's no need to borrow money, and even if you did, no one would care.

.⟨ NOW LOADING IN ⟩. TRACK TWO

"I had a horrible time riding a bus from Columbia to Washington, D.C. It involved rude people and an arrest." So read an e-mail from a reader. I could relate, having ridden a Greyhound from Columbia to Charleston, West Virginia, long ago. Drunks raised hell all night. To this day I'd rather sell than buy bus tickets. I know of what I speak. I worked as a ticket agent.

Athens, Georgia, 220 West Broad. Black smoke smudges the air as a red, white, and blue Greyhound revs up. That's my cue. I key the microphone: "Now loading in track two, Greyhound's local to Hull, Colbert, Comer, Carlton, Calhoun Falls, Saluda, Columbia, Fayetteville, Raleigh, and points north."

A clash of gears heralds the departure of another load of humanity. No sooner do they leave than a bus arrives, humanity spilling out. From morning to night the scene repeats.

I received a good education at 220 West Broad—a Ph.D. in life. Desperation, making do, dream chasing, and more were part of the curriculum, as were laughter and mean-spiritedness. In the bus station lobby I saw a man shoot himself. Wearing a soiled trench coat à la Lieutenant Columbo and bumbling à la Columbo, he approached the ticket counter. He dropped his gun.

Bam!

Shot in the leg and trailing blood, he limped out of the lobby. I found the mushroomed bullet in a corner. We never saw the blundering robber again.

One cold Saturday night two days before Christmas, M. E. Geer and I were closing the station. It was late and freezing. We had all the cash from the day's ticket and shipping fees, $7,000 or so, ready to go into the safe below the shipping counter. We each held several fat zipper-locked money pouches. Seven feet away was a heavy steel door we'd neglected to lock.

A wild-eyed hippie charged through. Gaunt, straggly bearded, with hair combed with a firecracker, he looked like an addict. Both hands were thrust into the pockets of his army field jacket. He pointed them right at us.

"Give me the bread, man."

We stared at him in disbelief. He slammed his concealed hands on the counter.

"Give me the bread, I'm in a hurry."

An eternity passed.

"C'mon! Give me the dough."

We each were about to hand over the money when this desperado said, "We've got a shipment of pizza dough here."

A huge flint rock propped the steel door open on warm days, and beyond the rock sat a dumpster, the receptacle of remnants of burgers a greaser and a bucktoothed girl peddled in the lobby grill.

One afternoon an agent came in to work the night shift.

"Some dude's in the dumpster."

We went out for a look. Feet wiggled in the air, a snorkeler in the islands. Agent Smith picked up the rock.

"Watch this."

He hurled it against the dumpster. The explosion deafened me. I can't imagine what it was like inside that steel chamber. The dumpster diver launched, a surface-to-air missile flying backwards, his hands morphed into rockets. He landed on his feet, running like a man on fire.

One cold January night, 10 degrees it was, a one-legged wino on oaken crutches hobbled over to the ticket counter.

"Mister you got something to drink?" He wasn't after coffee.

Half a bottle of cheap gin (purloined from an unlocked bag) had been gathering dust on a baggage shelf.

"Now don't drink it here," I told him.

"No, suh, I won't."

As soon as I handed it over, he drank it dry. We had him arrested. Later, feeling guilty, I took consolation in the fact that he had a warm place to sleep on a frigid night.

Some agents amused themselves going through unlocked baggage. What did they find? Reefer, cocaine, pills, pornographic materials, guns, and money. A vehicle of mass transit is a bad neighborhood on wheels.

Back then we used *Russell's Official Bus Guide* to plot routes and connections. With this thick, 1,000-page collection of all times and routes in the United States and Canada, we planned cross-country trips. This tedious process demanded that you keep many pages open, that you focus, and that you make notes, lots of notes. Screw up and a traveler would be stranded and you would hear about it. Worst of all, it meant you had to work. You could not walk across Hull Street to the Dawg House and drink beer and shoot pool on the clock.

Every ticket agent lived in fear of that one call where someone wanted to go from Athens to, say, Maple Bay, Washington. The accursed agent would be tied up for hours, plotting and making notes while the traveler patiently waited.

We visited this meanness on each other. One night the mark, Jimbo Wilson, a fellow always wanting us to work his shift, picked up the phone.

"Bus station."

Shielding the phone with his hand, he looked at us for pity. "Damn, this guy wants to go to Maple Bay, Washington."

"Ah, man, you're screwed."

True revenge is laughing well.

Ricky Wilson and Keith Strickland were baggage handlers. Ricky's sister, Cindy, stopped by often. They later met Fred Schneider and, along with Kate Pierson, formed the B 52s. Keith and I worked night shifts. Back then he was shy and soft spoken but destined to be a drummer turned guitarist and vocalist.

In the early 1970s guys grew their hair long, but Southeastern Stages' dress code banned long hair. One agent, Tony Gay, had extremely long, wavy, Led Zeppish hair. He refused to cut it. Instead, he tucked it into a hairnet and squeezed a short-haired wig over it. With his Roy Orbison glasses, Gene Shalit moustache, and wig, he was a sight for sore eyes.

One cold, windy March afternoon Mr. Strickland, the station manager, sent Tony to deposit the day's cash. Another agent spotted Tony walking up the street leaning into a strong wind. As he turned the corner at North Lumpkin, a March blast sent his wig scooting down the sidewalk like a large rat running for its life. Tony fell in hot pursuit. A policeman fell into the chase. It ended with a big laugh for all.

The pay was low, but the work was fun and revealing. Seeing all manner of humanity interact was eye opening. When I read the writer's account of her bus trip to D.C. and back, I knew what she had encountered.

Politicians, environmentalists, and people insulated from scalawags propose public transportation as a desirable way to move human beings about. If you like their idea, I suggest you get a job at a bus station. You are who you travel with. You'll soon agree that cars, freedom, and privacy make a combination that's hard to beat no matter what gas costs.

Working at that station was my last job as a blue-collar guy, and I miss the camaraderie I shared with its colorful characters. As at most places I've worked, white-collar stops included, most employees just wanted to have some fun and draw a check.

What became of the agents and porters I worked with? I never saw them again, but when I hear the B 52's "Love Shack" or see a red, white, and blue bus roar by I'm back at 220 West Broad in Athens, Georgia. I key an imaginary microphone and announce: "Now loading in track two, Greyhound's local to Hull, Colbert, Comer, Carlton, Calhoun Falls, Saluda, Columbia, Fayetteville, Raleigh, and points north." Then I remember the poor soul in the dumpster. I'm certain he never forgot his time at the bus station, either.

·⸨ LINCOLN STREET ⸩·

When you live far from your childhood home you see few reminders of your early years, but when you do it's startling. Just one word can ignite a firestorm of memories for you, the memoirist. One word, and memory's mystifying chemistry swirls the past and present into an amalgam of moments called life. For me, "Lincoln" ferries me across the river of time.

It's a spring day in Columbia. U.S.C. students jog by businessmen talking on cells. Standing at Gervais and Lincoln, I close my eyes and see my sixth-grade teacher, Helen Turner, leaning against her desk in Lincolnton, Georgia. She wears black-framed glasses, a white blouse, and a red skirt. She's reading a letter from a fellow sixth-grade class in Illinois. She laughs and crosses her lean legs. "These Northern students," she says, "can't believe a county in the Deep South took its name from Abraham Lincoln."

The historical marker at Gervais and Lincoln explains that Lincoln Street, like my home county, takes its name from Benjamin Lincoln. I know the story well. When a Southerner comes from a county named Lincoln he better know the details. Counties in Alabama, Georgia, Kentucky, Missouri, Tennessee, Vermont, and Maine took on General Benjamin Lincoln's name. Columbia and Savannah named streets after him. This glorious commemoration for Lincoln, who was a bit of a bureaucrat, surprises me. He lost most battles he participated in. His claim to fame is that he received General Cornwallis's sword of surrender at Yorktown.

This General Lincoln business aside, Lincoln Street is my favorite street in Columbia. It's bricked, and that gives it a cobblestone-like appearance. It feels a bit like Charleston. The Blue Marlin reinforces that impression. The restaurant sits where the old Seaboard Air Line Passenger Depot sat, once upon a time a train station/all-night diner that looked like an Edward Hopper painting. "Please pay when served" two signs over the counter beseeched. Just down the front-door steps was where I boarded the *Silver Star* that night in 1984. One night earlier I had walked into the old train station to buy tickets to Florida. The next evening, a fun-loving blonde, Linda, and I boarded Amtrak's *Silver Star* at 12:15. We were going to Deland to her sister's wedding.

Night riders, we were unsure what to expect. A few of the other travelers—nomads come to mind—joined us. Our chain of rolling steel pulled out of Lincoln Street and crept through town. We eased past a landmark where "ADLUH" glowed red, a place where men mill flour and cornmeal, occasionally giving away free biscuits. Momentum built, and soon city lights were no more.

We hurtled through darkened countryside, swaying side to side to a rhythmic clacking. Approaching crossings, the train would sing its forlorn song: two long blasts, a short blast, and a final long blast. Percussive clacking and airy weeping go the night-train anthem: how mournful in the dead of night, how lonely to those in blackened countryside lying in beds. Perhaps a few envy the travelers piercing their night. "To what magical places do they go?"

All the night, clacking conveyed me to another time and Steve Goodman's "The City of New Orleans." Arlo Guthrie transformed Goodman's lament into a 1972 hit. A train sounds its dirge-like notes with good cause. It's a goner. Darkness, doleful horns, sad strangers . . . altogether it's a requiem, for night riding upon steel wheels induces measured sadness. Whenever I hear a train in the dead of night I get the blues. Passenger trains have long been on the way out in the United States, and when you ride one you're riding out of—not into—history. Goodman knew this. He captured the beauty and loneliness of train travel.

We rocked through the night as upright passengers marked time like metronomes. We stopped in Savannah, and upheaval was on the way. A drunken woman boarded the train. She had an unruly head of hair and a rowdy temperament. She looked like a burnt-out go-go girl who long ago went-went one time too many. She was a businesslady. She went from man to man crying out, "My name is Mandy, and I have sweet candy."

She said she sang at a local bar in Savannah, this gypsy chanteuse. The conductor put her off at the next stop. And then all grew quiet but for the clacking of the wheels.

Our car—nowhere as poetic as a "magic carpet of steel"—rolled on, a rail-hugging bus crossing trestles and carrying drifters and a Georgia boy with no trust in his car. There was nothing to do but sit in the dark and gaze at a blur of ghostly trees and fields punctuated by yellow lights. Pale water shone as the *Silver Star* crossed rivers and swamps and the tips of estuaries. Perhaps alligators watched as we hurtled by, our diesel breath rattling palmetto fronds and streaming Spanish moss back like an old woman drying her hair.

We slowed, then came to a stop. I pressed my face against the window to see swirling phantoms fill the night. The *Silver Star* lurched from side to side. Just feet away the *Silver Meteor* roared by, bound for the Big Apple. We resumed our journey.

Before airliners filled the skies, before cars and Eisenhower's interstate system dominated travel, train was *the* way to go. Elegant dining and well-appointed coaches coddled the affluent. We, however, had nothing to eat as we sped toward the land of gators, oranges, manatees, and murderers, but it mattered little. I dreamed of streamliners and trains with names like *Hiawatha*, *Ferdinand Magellan*, *Zephyr*, and *Chief*.

Our journey ended in the Deland depot around 7:30 in the morning. It was there that déjà vu took hold. Across a large field sat noble locomotives along with a few rusting passenger coaches. A handsome locomotive, tan and dignified, sat out front at a 45-degree angle to a jumbled cluster of retired colleagues. A station attendant said some fellow was collecting them, providing a resting place for some of the 1930's great luxury trains. These grand old trains had shunted luminaries around these United States. Now they rested in a graveyard, and I thought of Goodman's song again.

We went to the wedding and my chief memory is hearing the bride's father describe the night he found an alligator on his front walkway. We rode the train back to Columbia, a trip I have no memory of, but I know we got off the train at Lincoln Street.

All these memories wash over me when I see the Lincoln Street marker. Lincoln Street. It sounds like a television series, and in a way it is. Every time I go to Lincoln Street, scenes and characters play in my mind.

Twenty-one years later, on a brilliant October afternoon, I was driving south on I-95 below Savannah. I glimpsed a distant trestle over golden marsh. "My name is Mandy and I have sweet candy." What happened to the unruly woman from Savannah? Dead, I'd bet. And Linda? We went our separate ways. And Helen Turner? Dead. And the glory days of streamliners and Zephyrs? Dead. And the couple we sent off honeymooning? Divorced. Steve Goodman? Dead. And old Dad's alligator? Dead. The Seaboard Diner? Closed.

No, they live on, and all it takes to summon them up is one word. Just one word. Lincoln.

·{ SACRED EARTH }·

The clay has kept us Catawba people. . . . We cannot let it die.

Caroleen Sanders

There's a secret spot up Lancaster way where digging uncovers thin shards 600 years old. Vessels once whole lie in ruin, and yet these remnants whisper to tribal members treading in the footsteps of ancient elders—*We are broken but not beaten. Make us whole again.*

Yes, broken but not beaten. Catawba pottery perseveres as one of South Carolina's more enduring art forms. And now, thanks to traditional Catawba potters, the old ways are returning.

Caroleen Sanders sits at a long, wooden table in the Native American Studies Center. Her tribal name is Night Moon. Stroking a communal peace pipe with a shard of agate, she gives it the polish some mistake as glaze. Catawba pottery, however, is never glazed. She's on a mission: to restore the Catawba pottery tradition.

"It's survived 4,000 years. We cannot let it die." As she applies deft strokes to the pipe, she talks about clay's role in maintaining the Catawba people, who had no choice but to intermix. "The clay has kept us Catawba people. That's who we are."

She stops polishing and reaches beneath the table. Out comes a cooking pot. A black snake coils around the top. A sunflower adorns the pot, too. "The snake wards off insects or whatever might be hungry and trying to get into the food pot," says Sanders. "I chose a black snake because it's so helpful to man."

And the sunflower? Well, she just loves 'em.

She used a sharp stone to crosshatch the snake's scales and a seashell to etch the sunflower into the clay. "I'm a person who likes detail," says Sanders.

The snake pot long existed somewhere along the Catawba River as unrefined clay, a natural resource.

"Catawba," you should know, means "People of the River," and their river is the Catawba, that thread of blue that rises in the Blue Ridge Mountains of western North Carolina and flows into Lake Wateree, where for all practical purposes it vanishes. But it leaves something magical, something sacred, behind. Clay.

Closely guarded secrets, the clay holes are not to be disclosed, not even photographed. "They're sacred," says Sanders. Once they dig a goodly amount of clay, potters refill the hole and camouflage it with brush and straw so that others can't find it.

The best clay is six feet down. "Finding a good seam of clay provides a rush like finding a vein of gold," says Sanders.

Catawba potters dig two types of clay: pan clay and pipe clay. The primary clay is the smooth pipe clay, which is used for smaller objects, ceremonial pipes for instance. Gritty pan clay is used as a strengthener and is mixed with pipe clay to make larger objects such as jars and cooking pots.

A distinguishing color of Catawba pottery is black. "You can dig in an area and get this black gunk, and that's from roots that have become a part of the clay," says Sanders.

Firing clay by coals yields black, too. First, though, the clay must be cleaned. "I let it sit there until it's soft, and I can rinse it around several times and pour all the water off until I can see blue, which is clay. When it's pliable, I start mixing it with my hand and squeezing and squeezing and squeezing it until I get enough that is liquid. Then I take a smaller bucket and I dig out what has been dissolved and pour it in another bucket, and I'll add more water and squeeze and squeeze and squeeze. It looks like a batter while I'm doing it."

The end product is very fine. Sanders strains it three times through three different types of material. "I can put my hand in a bucket once it's cleaned, and it looks like I have wax on my hand. I can do this [she holds her hands vertical], and it doesn't even run down."

Next is the making of pieces and all it entails: a vision, subject matter, the shaping, preparation for firing, firing, and color manipulation. Sanders fires her pieces around coals, just as her ancestors did. She likes to use fallen cedars (she never cuts cedars) but prefers red oak and hickory. Sanders carefully moves pieces in and away from the heat until they are able to withstand the fire. "I take the fire to the pieces, not the piece to the fire. You learn this by doing," she says. "That's the only way. Some people just put them in there and build a fire and let it rip and roar and leave it. But, honestly, when I'm taking my time to do a piece that I want to represent me in this mortal life, I want it to be something that's outstanding."

Sanders likes to create animals. One day she was firing a black turtle when she inadvertently gave it orange spots. "I was firing a turtle, and I wanted that turtle to be all black. So, I pulled it away from the coals and got my oak chips, not knowing that they had moisture in them."

Sanders poured oak chips over the turtle and left it. When she returned to get it, she was in for a surprise. "My black turtle had little orange specks on it. It looked like I had a real shell, one of the turtle shells that used to be black with a little orange."

Sanders would agree with what Chief William Harris, the chief of the Catawba Nation, told the House Interior Appropriations Subcommittee: "The tradition of pottery making among the Catawba, unchanged since before recorded history, links the lives of modern Catawba to our ancestors and symbolizes our connection to the earth and to the land and river we love." And she would agree with something else Harris said: "Like our pottery, the Catawba people have been created from the earth, and have been shaped and fired over time and so have survived many hardships to provide a living testament to our ancestors and to this place we call home."

Caroleen Sanders, born on the reservation, perpetuates her ancestors' connection with the earth. She's teaching others the old sacred earth ways but with a proviso. "They must have Catawba blood. This is a tradition that belongs to none other than the Catawba, and it's who we are and why we're still on the map today. And we treasure that."

THE COLONEL'S CAMELLIAS

Who's taking care of all those camellias now? The old Colonel has gone to that great camellia show in the sky. As I flip through the index cards in my memory under the category "Gardeners," there walks Colonel Parker Connor Jr. He lived in Mt. Pleasant for a time and, later, Greenville, but he once lived on Edisto Island at Oak Island Plantation. His great-great-grandfather William E. Seabrook built the plantation home in 1828. I was a guest there in 1993, a writer on assignment. My mission was to write about the colonel's unusual pastime. This story can best be appreciated over a glass of iced tea. So take a moment to pour a glass and read on.

The setting for Colonel Connor's avocation is classic. Oak Island Plantation sits at the end of a sandy road overlooking the Edisto marsh. The plantation home was long occupied by Connor's ancestors except for a stint during the Civil War when Union troops commandeered it. Colonel Connor told me the Union soldiers "liberated" the family's original furniture.

The house is stately and Southern through and through. The home, on the National Register of Historic Places, faces south across expansive reaches of salt marsh. "All the old Southern homes face south," said Connor. We walked the grounds that day, the Colonel and I, he ticking off the names of prized camellias . . . Dawn's Early Light, Boutonniere, Walterboro, and Wildwood.

How well I remember my time there. The calls of clapper rails drifted over the marsh, and the cries of pileated woodpeckers echoed through pines. The story of Oak Island Plantation, however, was not to be found in the pines, or in the Colonel's old mansion, or out in the marsh. Its story was about camellias, those plants that bloom as few others do: in late fall, winter, and early spring.

I suppose the Colonel tired of clashing metal, shouting commands, and war's brutality, this man who led infantrymen. His career included two tours in Germany and one in Korea. I imagine he grew weary of war machines and maneuvers. After retiring, in 1978, the Colonel turned to something peaceful—growing camellias. It took him only 15 years to go from the infantry to the top of the camellia world. In fact, he reigned as one of the Southeast's premiere camellia growers in the 1980s and 1990s.

As we walked that crisp January morning, he told me about his decision to retire, pointing at a nearby bloom and interjecting, "Dixie Night Supreme, gorgeous blooms." Some of his camellias, such as the Anemone and the Peony, are perfection. He had 400 varieties, and he routinely patrolled his camellia kingdom seeking the perfect bloom. He knew precisely what the judges looked for in a perfect bloom.

"Some judges like pink, some like red, some white, but perfection is what they look for," he said. He then launched into a description of an irreproachable, semi-double blossom. "If it's a semi-double, all the petals must be perfect, intact, standing up, and fresh. That'll win," he pronounced with an air of finality.

As we walked, I noticed several plants had swaths of green cheese-cloth wrapped around them. "To keep the infernal bees out," said the Colonel. "They can destroy a flower in two hours." The morning was cool. There were no bees. As if reading my mind, Colonel Connor continued. "You wait two hours," he said, "and you'll see a couple hundred bees on every bush in this yard. They pollinate the flowers, but they destroy the flower rooting around to get the pollen, kicking up their little feet like pigs in a trough. I would gladly get rid of the bees if I knew how. I'm an environmentalist but not that kind." No sooner had he said this than he pointed to a delicate blossom. "That's a Miss Charleston."

This plantation, with its ties to Connor's ancestors, its Civil War legacy, and its massive oaks, grows America's oldest camellia bush. "That big camellia over there under that oak was planted in 1830," said the Colonel. "It's probably the biggest one in the United States, 64 inches around its base."

The Colonel became interested in growing camellias by studying the history of the family plantation. He used to listen to his grandfather describe Oak Island Plantation as a showplace prior to the devastation of the Civil War. A formal English garden was laid out in 1830. It contained thousands of roses, and later Japanese gardeners built a water garden on the grounds.

The old grounds could have rivaled Middleton or Magnolia Gardens, those lowcountry jewels, Connor told me. But then "The War" came along and the family's fortune evaporated, leaving them penniless for some time. "Everything," said Connor, "went to rack and ruin."

It's interesting to speculate what might have come of Oak Island Plantation had there been no war. Perhaps it would have taken its place along celebrated lowcountry gardens where camellias are bright stars masquerading as native plants. They're not.

All this Southern camellia business came about as an accident of sorts. Truth be told, it comes down to deception. That tea you're supposed to be sipping: it's a cousin to camellias. Camellias and tea plants are in the same family. The Colonel told me how camellias came to the colonies.

"The British went to China to buy tea plants," said the Colonel, "and the Chinese fooled the British by selling them camellias instead." The Colonel went on to say he'd never heard of anyone making tea from the flowering camellia, but he "once heard about someone making some camellia wine." It doesn't sound palatable, certainly not like the tea we prize down South, which comes from *Camellia sinensis.*

After water, tea is the second most widely consumed beverage in the world. So enjoy your tea and be glad the British finally got hold of some real tea plants. Tea, you see, as Southern as it seems, came to us from China, courtesy of Britain.

And for the Colonel and other camellia enthusiasts, this cousin of the tea plant may not be potable, but it brings joy of another sort: beautiful splashes of color in a season known for cool, dark days. And, more than that, it brings something better, a colorful way to compete without guns, sabers, and artillery.

Colonel Connor died June 26, 2013, almost 20 years after we walked the camellia-strewn grounds of Oak Island Plantation. His funeral was held July 1 in the Presbyterian Church on Edisto Island. His service received full military honors. I don't think it's possible to get camellias in the heat of summer, but I like to think his family somehow got those ravishing flowers of winter. I like to think that a blanket of red-and-white Dixie Night Supremes and blue sasanquas overlay the casket of this veteran of 29 years, a military man who waged war against those infernal bees.

Across Georgialina aspiring artists painted Coca-Cola advertisements over many a small-town wall, creating a latter-day market for Coke nostalgia.

PHOTOGRAPH BY ROBERT C. CLARK.

❧ RECOLLECTION ❧

Recalling the old ways resurrects a mysterious time. All manner of wizards helped people face life's challenges. Folks dug their own wells by hand, and I recall Dad talking about a man who used a dogwood branch to help people divine water's whereabouts.

A man took a wart off my thumb using broomstraw. I remember, too, hearing my grandparents talk about how people would sit up all night with the dead. Mom recalls how evenings rang with lovely melodies as bell cows made their way from one pasture to another.

People who came out of the Depression remained thrifty throughout life. As Granddad Walker told me, "It doesn't matter how much money you make. What matters is how much you keep." My Aunt Evelyn remembers trading eggs during the Depression to get things they needed and how women made dresses from flour sacks.

When I was growing up, the weekly newspaper supplied me with personal news, old saws, and community events. And on rare occasion that little newspaper covered a rare event, a snowfall. We got news, too, about communities like Danburg and what our neighbors were up to. Some communities didn't survive, though, strangled to death by progress. Who today remembers what it was like before air-conditioning came along? Beating the heat took ingenuity, and it didn't hurt if you had a high tolerance for the upper end of

Fahrenheit's scale. We all have that one teacher we remember. How sad to pay tribute after they die, but better late than never.

Come winter we Southern kids dreamed of snow. What a magical time that was. You woke up and there it was. Recollection—it's a beautiful thing.

THE SMALL-TOWN WEEKLY

Growing up, I don't recall being short for news. We had a daily newspaper, the *Augusta Chronicle*, a few radio stations, and for a long time two TV stations. We got plenty news from beyond the county. What we didn't get every day, except through the grapevine, was news about our neighbors, the people of Lincoln County. That's what made Thursdays so special to those of us who lived outside the town limits. The *Lincoln Journal* arrived.

Every Thursday, farmers, grandmothers, country storeowners, and a host of others pulled news about people we knew from their mailboxes.

The *Journal* continues to deliver much-needed news, and it has grown up a lot since those days of personals and quaint ads and notices. You can get the *Journal* in color over the Internet, but you'll miss the rustle of paper and the faint smell of ink.

Today, it exhibits a much more sophisticated approach to local news and happenings, but I remember how it used to be. Thanks to a subscription from my parents, I received the *Journal* for many years.

I remember the personals the most. Reading columns such as "Hoots from the Holler," I could get a feeling for the social calendar even though I lived more than 100 miles away. "The Smiths ate Sunday dinner with the Joneses. It was delicious." "The Browns drove through the Smokies. The leaves were beautiful." Remember those quaint notices?

If the personals celebrated friendship, the classifieds underscored peoples' connection to the land. "Pens for sale for hunting dogs." "Trailer for hauling livestock to market." "Hunting land for lease."

And, of course, advertisements from local eateries. "Ribs: All You Can Eat."

All that good food in unlimited amounts created a need for other ads hawking products. Apparently, patrons' waistlines suffered the cumulative effects of "all-you-can-eat" deals. I remember how an advertisement for the Comf-O-Mate Extender promised relief. "For $3.50 you can attach it to your jeans, pants, or skirt and extend the waistline a whole inch, *when you need it.*" (I suspect you needed it most when sitting too long in an all-you-can-eat restaurant.)

If the Comf-O-Mate got to be a bit of an embarrassment, another advertisement might provide a solution for those determined to drop a few pounds. "Go-bese" tablets (what wordplay!), available at one of the two local drug stores, offered a way, perchance, to reduce that bulging waistline.

Two things you could always expect to see. If it snowed, some fellow up town would stick a ruler into the snow and the headline would proclaim the number of inches of that magical stuff we got. In spring the *Journal* always ran a photo of Mr. Clifford with the turkey gobbler, long beard and all, that "he killed somewhere down yonder." He took his secret hunting ground to the grave with him.

For sure, those days were simpler times. I remember when people would buy advertising space and run an "engraved" invitation to the entire county to their daughter's wedding. It was a pragmatic, if not sophisticated, solution to a need.

Weddings, accidents, church socials, funerals, football championships, and grand jury indictments made for copy more compelling than anything on the national stage. Every page of every issue, true to life in the South, revealed things that genuinely mattered to local readers. Community life, planting and harvesting, babies, birthday parties, and golden anniversaries provided dependable, interesting reading. Who's in the hospital, who's out, and who has passed away reminded us that time and good health are true gifts never to be taken lightly.

Obituaries, a staple of papers small and large, then as now, ran with verses accompanying photographs of the dearly departed. When children died, a carefully selected, heartfelt passage occasionally resurrected memories of James Agee's "Shady Grove, Alabama, July 1936," a beautiful description of a cemetery in the classic book

Let Us Now Praise Famous Men. Agee closes his description with the sentiment parents had engraved on the back of the headstone bearing their six-month-old daughter's likeness.

"We can't have all things in life that please us. Our little daughter, Jo Ann, has gone to Jesus."

Then as now, the reading was sad in that little paper of our own. At other times funny, useful, and always interesting in its steady delivery of news, maxims, and personal items. "After church, we enjoyed squash, potato salad, fried chicken, collards, and tea."

The historian Avery Craven wrote that reading Southern country newspapers was like "sitting down to a meal of turnip greens, black-eyed peas and corn bread, with a glass of buttermilk on the side." I agree. You were always in for good, down-home enlightenment.

Weekly papers amount to history books, too. They serve as valuable repositories of heritage, stories, changing times, laws, weddings, divorces, and births and deaths. They recorded olden times, too.

During the sunset of his life, my Grandfather Walker wrote a letter to the *News Reporter* in Washington, Georgia. He wanted to record the stories his grandmother had passed down to him: how to break a dog of chasing sheep by roping it to a large ram that would drag it about, how a farmer kept Union troops from eating his smoked hams by damming a creek and burying them so the creek would cover them once the dam was broken. And he recalled that difficult time, Reconstruction.

We still care about the same things my grandfather's grandparents did: community, making a living, educating children, doing something about crime, and knowing what our neighbors and friends are up to.

I remember pulling a yellowed copy of the *Lincoln Journal* off my parent's coffee table and looking it over pretty good back in the late 1970s. I remember thinking things are changing. Ads for huge satellite dishes and mobile phones and colored grocery store inserts looked oddly out of place in the *Journal.*

A closer look, however, revealed that my hometown newspaper remained reassuringly the same. Atop the front page, the masthead still proclaimed *The Lincoln Journal* in large type. No glasses needed to read that. In the upper right corner sat a sketch of the Courthouse. Beneath the paper's name rung out a bit of wisdom as it still does. "To thine own self be true, and it must follow, as the night the day, Thou canst not be false to any man." This saying, evocative of Bible verses, is actually a line spoken by Polonius in Shakespeare's *Hamlet.*

I know that weekly newspapers like ours aren't limited to the South, but I believe the best ones are here. These little papers reveal the South's steadfast heart. They mirror our hopes, fears, likes, dislikes, and daily concerns all packaged and presented on a weekly basis. They keep us in touch with our neighbors, old classmates, and family. And in some distant time historians who dig into them will discover nuggets and gems as valuable as those that came out of California's 1849 gold fields.

·{ MAGIC WAS }· IN THE AIR

If anything could top an idle day of summer fishing and playing in the creeks, it was snow. What made snow such an antithesis to summer heat was its capricious nature. The Information Age had yet to materialize, and in those uncomplicated days we had no Weather Channel to tell us days in advance that snow was coming. It either came or it didn't, and most of time, living in eastern Georgia and far from the mountains as we did, it didn't. But when it did, well, it provided joy like no other weather can.

Magical mornings. My parents would wake me up. "Look out the window."

There it was! A winter wonderland rare and sublime. There it was, that crystalline miracle, snow. Gold dust might as well have fallen during the night. Adrenalin surged through me. Mere sleeping had transported me to the land of the midnight sun and ice and snow. An altogether new architecture redefined all that was familiar into white lines and soft, glistening curves. It was as if a milky species of kudzu had carpeted the county.

Soon my sisters and I were marring the perfect surface with our tracks. (I always hated making tracks on that smooth, crystalline surface. I was ruining the only perfect thing I'd known. But out the door we went.)

On those rare, snow-blanketed mornings I happened to awaken first, I could tell something was different. The world seemed muted: a strange, soft silence muffled morning. A distant car seemed to slush down the Augusta Highway. And then I'd notice that the light seeping around the blinds and curtains seemed bluish. Peeking through the window, I got a jolt. Snow had fallen throughout the night.

Memories of childhood snows live within me still. Those snows of childhood held magic. Few things rival the spellbinding beauty of quarter-sized flakes cartwheeling through the air. Mesmerized by their fall, I knew that nothing but good could come from flakes like that. No school. A snowman. A friendly snowball fight. Snow ice cream! Just skim a layer off the car roof into a bowl, mix in sugar, vanilla extract, and milk and, voilà, ice cream!

Freshly fallen snow meant a chance to walk through dead-quiet wintry woods that seemed more like Vermont than Georgia to me, though I had never been to Vermont. But there with the boughs crusted white, limbs sporting a meringue of white and creaking a bit, and the ground softly cloudlike, the woods behind home seemed Vermont-like. As I walked through the trees, my boots crunched and squeaked, a deafening noise in that dampened winter wonderland.

Suddenly the creatures of the woods revealed themselves in a way like no other. Tracks galore. Dad and I once tracked a rabbit down until we found it sitting as still as stone, melding into a patch of brown leaves so perfectly that seeing it came as a total shock. Raccoon tracks and birds did their part to stencil wintry wildlife patterns onto the snow. A snowfall reveals evidence of the denizens of woods and fields like no other phenomenon. It's a powdery lab where biology refuses to be ignored.

A snowfall made for a time of adventurous survival, too. Those rare days of childhood snow sometimes knocked out the power. That meant tomato soup warmed over gas space heaters, wet clothes, and freezing hands and toes. And even that misery held its own peculiar brand of joy.

All those magical winter moments live in a place called recollection. To this day, snow unleashes a medley of memorable experiences in childhood, and the remarkable thing is that those memories retain their magic forever. As I write, I see a nine-year-old boy, Tommy, donning a cheap parka and gloves. Soon his fingers will burn from snow's icy flames, but he won't care.

Dad, as many dads did in the fifties, bought a Bell & Howell 8 millimeter camera and made home movies. To this day, I can see the snowfall he captured on film; I want to say it's the winter or late spring of 1958. I do believe it's April. Our dog, Duke, romps in the snow. Mom holds up a handmade sign giving the date and I believe the snow's depth of eight inches. The film jerks and swings wildly. Suddenly someone else is filming and my father runs into the camera: red from the cold, his heavy 5 o'clock shadow evident. Closer he comes, his face near the lens. Mom always said that shot made him look like an escaped convict. He was but 32 years old. He was a boy playing in the snow. Snow makes children of us Southerners. That's its true beauty.

Snow today? It means a hassle for those who drive to work. Over here in the city, as traffic snarls and fender benders break out like some metallic rash, area body-shop owners anticipate a windfall of sorts.

Well before the snow arrives (it usually doesn't), schools start giving notice that there'll be a three-hour delay the next morning or, even better to the kids, no school at all. But generally all that happens is that a huge front of disappointment moves through. You could say a depression settles in 'cause every kid's spirit plummets when snow fails to materialize.

It's just a fact of life. Southern weathermen today are no good at predicting snow. Whenever a weatherman says it's a certainty snow is coming, I know it's not. But that doesn't stop people from making a run on bread, milk, and soup at all the grocery stores. As soon as weathermen, those new celebrities born of clouds and climate, predict snow, people rise up like a horde of locusts and strip the shelves bare.

I can't speak for you, but I much prefer the old days when a blanket of snow, thin though it might be, would catch us by surprise. You'd wake up and there it would be, covering the land, an unanticipated veneer of confectioner's sugar.

The allure of the exotic and the magic of discovery I guess are where the joy of snow came from in my youth.

Things changed, sadly. Now it's unwise to eat snow ice cream. The air is filled with toxic particles, pollution, and other particulates that put snow ice cream on the "do not eat" list. Thanks a lot, progress.

And driving in the snow amounts to a demolition derby down here where it doesn't snow enough to justify snow plows. When it does snow, some Northern transplants like to make fun of us, both our unbridled glee and our traffic troubles. "My Gawd, it's just a little snow." (Perhaps some of you recall the July 1995 heat wave that struck up North. In Chicago, 525 people died. "My God, it was just a little heat.")

Is there a chance we'll have a record snow like the one that hit in 1973? I don't know, and I am doubly sure weather forecasters don't know. Here's hoping the so-called weathermen get it right just once this winter. Give the kids some snow, but do us a favor. Don't predict snow. If you and your learned ways and satellites know for sure snow is coming, don't forecast it. Let a new generation of children experience the magic of a surprise Southern snowfall.

For your children's' sake, I hope they go to bed one winter night dreading a test at school the next day. And then, throughout the night, here they come: fluffy alabaster flakes tumbling to earth, a soft whispering accompanying their fall. Early the next morning, the world seems bluish and quiet.

And then Dad or Mom or both come into the bedroom. "Look out the window."

A day of magic, one the kids will remember the rest of their lives, is about to unfold.

·{ REMEMBERING DANBURG }·

Ecologists love remnant habitats, where time has yet to ruin what nature so carefully assembles. We can thank isolation for pockets of remnant habitats. The modern world has passed them by and has forgotten they exist. Here and there you can also find remnant habitats for man: communities of the past. Danburg is such a place. Just glance at the map and you see that Danburg sits off the beaten path. If you pass through Danburg you are lost or go there for a reason.

One bright November afternoon Mom and I drove to Danburg, Georgia, to see places she knew as a girl. That drive transported us to a time when Danburg was far more than a country crossroads. It was a place where people prospered. It lives in isolation today with reminders of former glory and family here and there.

Many times Mom's mentioned this spot in the road that's more than a spot in the road. "Historic hamlet" comes to mind. The Confederate gold train came through here. Along that road, Highway 44, sits an old home referred to as the Matthews Farm Place. This circa 1910 Victorian home is no ordinary home. The doctor who delivered Mom, Dr. McNeil, lived there at the time she was born. Down its driveway he went to bring my mother into the world. And now we both were back, remembering those long ago days.

Dr. McNeil would have passed the Pink Anderson house, a place Mom remembers well though she never went inside. This stately home on the National Register of Historic Places is a Greek Revival home. It most likely incorporates an earlier building Dr. W. D. Quinn erected in the 1790s. So says the research. John Anderson later built the home as it appears today. The home's columns came from Savannah, the mirrors and cornices from England. New York and Chicago provided the home's fine furniture and curtains. A 24-by-35-foot banquet room and stone kitchen stood in a separate building connected to the main home by a breezeway.

The last Anderson to live in the home was Miss Pink Anderson, thus my mom's reference to the place as the Pink Anderson home. Miss Pink lived there during the Great Depression. Money was beyond tight, and the formal gardens and fountain vanished as vines and undergrowth took over.

The home sat empty for many years until 1962 when Mom's Uncle Ernest Walker bought it and remodeled it. The roof of the old kitchen and dining room had fallen in, leaving the walls standing. Down they came, demolished.

Richard Simms bought the home in 1972, adding a porch in the back. Research says too that Vinnie and Roderick Dowling now own this old home. It's beautiful. A large holly and magnolia contend for space, and both conspire to hide one of the columns gracing the home. A classic white picket fence fronts the building, which faces Highway 44.

Danburg is quaint and, it turns out, difficult to research. Stymied and a bit frustrated, I received some suggestions and phone numbers. I made a few calls. One led to Robert "Skeet" Willingham, who's written the history of Wilkes County. We had a lively talk about Danburg, a unique monument, and two old stores.

"Those old stores shut down twenty-five to thirty years ago," said Skeet. The two abandoned stores face each other at a slight angle near the Pink Anderson house. An old gas pump graces one store that sits on stacks of bricks. Its old Erie pump, eaten up with rust, last rung up gas at 31 cents a gallon. "Mr. Major operated that store," said Skeet. In the window of the other store is an old advertisement for Winston Super Kings. Strangely enough, sunlight has not faded the ad. It appears as if were printed yesterday.

Close by the store stands a monolith, but no ordinary monument. Each side of the monolith pays tribute to a group of people, some of whom were in direct conflict. One side honors veterans of World Wars I and II, Korea, and Vietnam. "Our debts to these veterans are equally vast, for their sacrifices were too often undervalued by the public at the very time they were made." Another side honors "black citizens of the village." Carved into the blue granite are these words: "Entrapped involuntarily in a system of servitude until 1865. They were thereafter entangled with the white citizens in a system of cotton-tenant-farming that exploited both through 1945 for the advantage of northern industrial capitalism. Both bondages were born by the black citizens with incredible fortitude, patience and humor."

Another side honors the memory of antebellum and Confederate leaders. "If their ideal of slavery was undoubtedly unjust, the quality of their public service was superb." The monolith's slanting desk-like top honors the families who settled near Danburg. A final side is dedicated to the memory of the vanquished British loyalists of 1776.

Skeet said that Danburg native John Boyd directed the creation of this monument, which was chiseled from Elbert County blue granite. "Boyd was a top executive of an insurance company in Jacksonville," said Skeet. "He loves history and wanted to record and honor it."

Danburg was a well-educated and sophisticated community that took its name from a New Englander, Samuel Danforth, the town's first postmaster. The original spelling was "Danburgh," but the "h" was dropped. The first name for the community was Newford, as in nearby New Ford Creek. An aside—my Granddad Walker said he had heard that the Confederate gold had been buried in Newford Creek, yet another twist to this tale of lost gold, yet another thread of history in the tapestry that is Danburg's.

Beyond the monolith sits the Danburg Baptist Church. Mom and I walked through its cemetery. We found the grave of cousin Clara Rhodes Blackmon, who died in 1989. She was born in 1897, which would make her close to sixty by the time I was old enough to be a smart aleck. I don't recall the lady, but Mom said she liked to be firm with misbehaving children and she always got in the last word. The story goes that I, having been in a blackberry patch, had picked up some chiggers. And chiggers, being the irritating critters they are, were giving me a hard time you know where. Being a mere boy, I did what boys do. I had my hand down there scratching away. Cousin Clara, upon seeing my shameful behavior, reprimanded me.

"Boy, just what do you think you are doing!"

Without missing a beat I responded, "I have a little bird here that goes tweet, tweet, tweet. Do you want to see it?"

Mortified, Cousin Clara said not one word. Looking at her stone, I thought about that day and I recalled a stout lady. I could see her with her hand over her mouth, stunned into silence.

Farther down from the Danburg Baptist Church sits the original Newford Baptist Church. "An architectural treasure," said Skeet. He explained that it has an early Victorian porch construction, which renders it less modest than most churches.

As day wore on the brilliant blue November sky darkened. As blue shadows crept over fields and roadways, we turned toward Beulah Church, where we walked its cemetery.

Later, as we drove into Lincolnton, I spotted a classmate, Dwain Moss, and his wife, Pat, raking leaves in the yard of Miss Azalean Wansley's old home. Miss Wansley taught me in the fifth grade, and I clearly could see her old mint-green Chevrolet in the yard where we stood. 'Twas the only car she owned. We turned around and chatted with Dwain and Pat. Much of our talk centered on how sad it was that so many of the county's historic buildings have been lost.

Dwain writes about Lincoln County's history, and talking with him provided a fitting end to an afternoon devoted to the past. Contemporary life easily deflects us from times gone by, but the past is patient, and it waits for those few souls willing to visit it. I was glad to have such a fine day with Mom.

Connecting with the past isn't a bad way to spend an afternoon. In fact, it's a great way to better understand what our parents and grandparents experienced in their youth. We are all just passing through, and we'll be gone far longer than we are here. It's comforting to think that someday when we are long gone our descendants will pay us a visit and for a fleeting moment memories thought lost will awaken. Other Danburgs are out there. Lets hope our children don't forget that they exist.

·❳ BEATING ❲· THE HEAT

The lyrics from the Lovin' Spoonful's "Summer in the City" resonate down South. Does it get hot here? Well, here's how climatologists describe Georgia: "A humid subtropical climate with mild winters and hot moist summers is characteristic of most of Georgia." Here's how I describe a hot summer day in Georgia: "A searing Georgia afternoon is like sitting on a Broilmaster grill in one of those massive ovens that bakes enamel paint onto cars. The air is thick, toxic almost, and you can't breathe. A starched white oxford shirt sticks to your skin, which is close to melting. Your shoes feel like they're filled with coals, and the nearest drink of water is 100 miles away."

When the temperature climbs into the high 90s and beyond and the humidity feels like it comes from a steam iron, Georgia and South

Carolina get hot. So hot it makes me wonder how folks got through those long summer days and evenings before air-conditioning arrived. Old homes were built with large windows and high ceilings and that helped, but it had to be brutal.

I remember one particularly sweltering summer day when I was a boy. I checked the record highs for Georgia and that day occurred the summer of 1955. The mercury reached a scorching 107 in Augusta in July 1955. (Three years earlier, on July 24, 1952, the folks in Louisville reached a record high for the state, 112 degrees Fahrenheit, a record that was tied August 20, 1983, in Greenville.)

Today we beat the heat with high-powered Carriers, Rheems, Tranes, and Lennox air-conditioners. Freon, ozone problems or not, stands as one of man's great achievements, and if you don't think so, drive around with no AC. Chlorine-free Puron has replaced Freon-based R-22 and it doesn't destroy the ozone layer. So, strike a medal for Puron's inventor, too.

But how did we cope with the heat before air-conditioning? I'll forego the old swimming hole cliché. Instead, I offer up five ways we survived.

Homemade ice cream. Kudzu. Fans. Icy Coca-Colas. Freezer lockers.

How well I remember the excitement that gripped me when I saw Mom and Dad slicing peaches late on a Sunday afternoon. Mom, reaching for the vanilla extract, would make the ice cream mix, and in went those peaches, nuggets of gold floating in liquid snow. Sometimes she added cherries, sometimes strawberries, and sometimes it was just plain vanilla ice cream. Always it was fabulous and a relief from the heat.

Dad never had to tell me twice to churn the ice cream. I was on it. I'd crank away. He'd add Morton's rock salt to the water, making a chilling brine within which the six-quart canister turned, occasionally lodging up against an ice chunk. And what boy doesn't remember the Morton salt girl in the yellow dress carrying an umbrella? "When It Rains It Pours."

I'd churn away, and the churning would get harder and harder. As the churn slowed, my sisters, Brenda and Deb, drew closer. When we saw ice cream oozing out of the top, it was ready, and off they ran. Dad would come take out the canister and give it to Mom. She'd scrape cream from the blade, and soon we were feasting on cold bowls of homemade ice cream. If you didn't get brain freeze eating home-made ice cream, you weren't eating it right.

Many a hot evening, often on Sundays, we'd have homemade ice cream and it didn't matter if the mercury topped 100; we felt like it was 40 degrees!

One of the darkest days in humanity was the invention of the elec-tric ice cream churn. Some things are meant to be done by hand, and churning ice cream is one of them. But then someone got the bright idea of adding an electric motor to the churn, and what a racket it makes, whining and grinding away.

Another way to beat the heat was with kudzu. That's right, kudzu. My Grandfather Walker would string a lattice of hemp among the columns on his front porch and plant kudzu at their base. In short order a dense, deep green screen of kudzu blocked out the sun. It felt 20 degrees cooler behind that buffer of greenery. What I remem-ber too is the pure quality of light hitting those broad green leaves. The kudzu glowed in an emerald-translucent way that made you feel cooler just by looking at it.

Another great invention was the window fan and its cousin, the box fan. For a long time I couldn't sleep without a nearby window fan purring away. The white noise of the fan's blades moving air proved soothing, and the cool air flowing over my skin made it easier to sleep. On a blistering night when you hoped a thunderstorm would come crashing through but heat lightning was all you got, you could get by with a window fan, something you don't see as much these days.

It had to be that brutally hot day in July 1955 when Dad went into town and bought a box fan. He brought it home, and we put trays of ice cubes in front of it. We sat so the wind could blow over the ice right at us. Wind hinting of ice cubes was as good as it got.

Another heat buster was an icy Coca-Cola from an old-timey box filled with water and hard chunks of glass-like ice, not that frothy airy ice you see today. If you reached in deep to get a Coke off the bot-tom, your arm went numb and your fingers tingled.

The best Coke I ever had was on my Granddad Poland's farm when I was a boy. Aunt Vivian went up to Price's Store to get Cokes for all of us. We had been gathering hay beneath a fiery sun. I was sitting against a persimmon tree on a hill overlooking the hayfield when Aunt Vivian handed me a cold Coke, condensation dripping from it. As long as I live, I'll remember my first draw on that Coke. It burned all the way down, and my body shed about 18 degrees of heat in two swallows.

Another way to cool off was to open the freezer locker and lean into it. I've never been to the Arctic, but I can't imagine drier, colder air. Dense clouds of vapors rose as I opened the door. Leaning over, I'd inhale that chill air. It smelled cold and clean, and from the first moment I breathed deeply the heat left me. All the frost on frozen tomatoes and vegetables looked like frozen tundra, and for a brief interlude I had miraculously flown from the steamy latitude of 33.824 to the North Pole.

Eating homemade ice cream, drinking teeth-shattering Coca-Colas, sitting near fans, standing behind a cool screen of kudzu, and immersing myself in the Arctic via the frosty breath of a freezer locker: that's how I kept cool as a boy. I was doing more than surviving the heat. I was storing great memories of a time when we found innovative ways to cool off.

Today's kids walk into an air-conditioned house, ride in an air-conditioned car, and drink Cokes from an air-conditioned box. They probably think kudzu is some new video game. I don't even know if kids today know what homemade ice cream is. Something you get at Baskin-Robbins, I suppose. If that's true, what a shame. They may be cool, but they don't know what they're missing, do they?

·} THE GREAT DEPRESSION'S LONG SHADOW {·

"We were so poor Mama would bleach the coffee grounds and serve 'em as grits the next morning." The Great Depression was no joking matter to the people who experienced it.

I'm too young to remember those dark days, but I've heard about them from my mom and others. The Great Depression left several generations with indelible memories.

One Georgia woman remembers how her family made a stepladder into a Christmas tree. They wrapped tissue paper around the ladder and placed candles upon the steps. They could light them only now and then or they'd burn up before Christmas day. She has no memory of any toys come Christmas, just homemade gloves and scarves. Things that helped them weather the winter.

Back then people had no money to buy dishes, so companies gave away "depression glass." There was, however, plenty of heartbreak to go around. Said one man, "My daddy was the strongest man I know, but the Depression brought him to his knees."

People who endured the Depression learned lifelong lessons. Granddad Walker told me something I never forgot. "It doesn't matter how much money you make," he said. "What matters is how much you keep."

Yes, what you managed to hang onto mattered, but holding on was near impossible. The boll weevil's devastation greased the way for the Great Depression. Many farmers abandoned their land. Banks took it—if they hadn't failed.

People went hungry. It makes one dredge up Scarlett O'Hara's infamous lines, a reference to how Union troops marched through Georgia scorching anything remotely resembling food. "As God is my witness, they're not going to lick me. I'm going to live through this and when it's all over, I'll never be hungry again. No, nor any of my folk. If I have to lie, steal, cheat, or kill. As God is my witness, I'll never be hungry again."

During the Depression, a biscuit was a banquet come Sundays. Some good came from the misery, though.

Aunt Evelyn remembers how people stuck together and made do. "We didn't eat eggs; we bartered them for things we didn't have. It was a time when everybody had dresses made from bolts of cloth provided by the WPA so everybody looked alike." She remembers wearing dresses made from flour sacks, which she had had to wash over and over to get the numbers and printing out.

Aunt Evelyn and Mom remember working hard as children. "On Saturdays," Aunt Evelyn said, "we'd dig up white dirt [kaolin] and whitewash the fireplaces and chimneys, and brush the yards with bresh brooms to clean up behind the chickens."

She remembers how neighbors helped each other. "We shared a good garden with those whose garden failed. Daddy would kill a beef every year. He'd put it in a wagon and take it to the neighbors and share part of it. When they killed a beef they did the same thing. So everyone had some beef that way."

How the times have changed. We live in a throwaway society now. People throw away things today that Depression-era sufferers would consider treasure. Granddad Poland had a saying: "Keep something seven years, and you'll find another use for it." That philosophy trickled down to Dad, who kept things ranging from heaps of tangled metal, broken equipment, and lumber scraps to PVC pipe. Someday he'd need it.

I wonder what the ghosts of front-line Depression-era folks think today. On every corner they see a fast-food restaurant. They see well-fed people so overweight they struggle to get out of their cars. They see people wearing a dazzling array of clothes and holding strange contraptions to their ears while they talk to themselves. What might these phantoms think of us? I think I know; I bet you do, too.

Life hammered a realistic outlook into the psyches of the people who came from the Depression. They clung to what worked and they passed their proven beliefs and knowledge on. Some survivors' children hold those same virtues today. They're not about self-indulgence and the immediate gratification material things offer. And that's a lesson we all could benefit from, if only we stop long enough to reflect and absorb it.

As surely as fire tempers steel, hard times shape people's character. Though the Depression's long in our rearview mirrors, we owe these people belated respect. They received no bailouts. They simply picked up and survived.

·{ WE CALLED }· HIM KILGO

Spring quarter at UGA in Athens, Georgia. A windy morning. Dogwood petals blow about. James Kilgo, in a blue-and-white seersucker suit, is reading from William Faulkner's "The Bear." Isaac McCaslin is lost in deep woods when a pivotal moment occurs. "And the wilderness coalesced," read Kilgo as I glanced over my shoulder through a dogwood-shaded window to see Peggy Culbertson walking up the sidewalk. It was a beautiful juxtaposition: two passions—our high school beauty and English literature—merge amid a flurry of dogwood petals. But other things made English 102 memorable, chiefly James Patrick Kilgo.

Kilgo had auburn hair and an auburn beard, and he cut a striking figure in those seersucker suits. His eyes held fire. Not one moment in his classroom was devoted to tedium, and yet I made a miserable showing.

All those years ago, little did I know that coincidences, parallels, and connections with Kilgo would occur in the decades ahead. I was sitting in James Dickey's living room in 1989 when Dickey mentioned a book. "I read a book I like a lot. The title had something to do with ivory bills."

"*Deep Enough for Ivorybills*," I said. "James Kilgo wrote it."

"He's good," said Dickey.

Deep Enough for Ivorybills began as a column for the Athens *Banner-Herald* in which Kilgo shared hunting, fishing, and outdoor stories from the Pee Dee swamps of Darlington County, South Carolina. Rewritten in book form, the columns reveal his hunt for a place in the soul and heart spacious enough for beauty and mystery—a sanctuary deep enough for ivorybills.

Kilgo didn't write creatively until he was in his thirties. I remembered how Faulkner inspired Kilgo. I recall, too, that he loved the opening lines to Isak Dinesen's *Out of Africa*, calling them "sublime." Even now I see him cock his head back and read: "I had a farm in Africa, at the foot of the Ngong Hills."

Our paths converged. In the 1980s I served as the managing editor for *South Carolina Wildlife* magazine. Years after I left, Caroline Foster took that position. Her uncle? Jim Kilgo.

Our paths tightened. In 1995, just four years before Kilgo retired, he taught my daughter, Becky. Daughter and father—on opposite sides of his continuum—shared a connection, and we agreed he was unforgettable.

One evening as the sun dropped, I read Kilgo's book *The Blue Wall—Wilderness of the Carolinas and Georgia*. Kilgo collaborated with the photographer Thomas Wyche to write a book about my beloved Georgialina, a Southland. Yet another connection.

The only time I saw him after that course long ago in Athens was at the South Carolina Festival for Books. It was March 22, 1997. I brought *Deep Enough for Ivorybills*, which he inscribed "To Tom with memories of good times at UGA."

I brought, too, *The Blue Wall*, in which he wrote, "For my friend and former student, Tom Poland—those splendid hills—warm regards, Jim."

He was looking forward to retiring so that he could devote more time to writing. He said life had conspired at every turn to rob him of the time he needed to write. A short while later I bumped into Caroline Foster, who told me of his passing. Life's conspiracy had robbed him all right. He retired in 1999 and died three years later. The trail didn't end there, however.

Kilgo reached from the grave to touch me again. Robert Clark and I were spending an afternoon with the wildlife sculptor Grainger McKoy in the spring of 2012. Upon hearing I had graduated from Georgia, McKoy asks, "Did you know Jim Kilgo?"

McKoy hands me a lavish booklet, "The Brilliance of Birds." It features Grainger's work and an essay by James Kilgo, "The Art of Grainger McKoy." Kilgo had sat in the same chair I was in when McKoy handed me "The Brilliance of Birds." I felt an irresistible pull back to that classroom and the fluttering dogwood petals.

I doubt any of what I'm writing matters to you, the reader, but it does to me. You see, as much as I loved Kilgo's English 102 course, I earned only a C. I'd like for Jim to know that I figured things out, but because that was impossible I did the only thing left. I went to his swamps and forests, the ones deep enough for ivory-billed woodpeckers.

October 2012. Robert Clark and I are exploring Darlington County swamps fringing the Pee Dee River. We follow a band of horsemen in my all-wheel-drive Honda. We go past silky green waters where snakes weave serpentine paths through duckweed. When we can drive no more we trudge through tangled undergrowth. We dodge cypress knees that would trip us. Deeper and deeper we go, fighting off vines and shrubs. We pass a cemetery so old its tombstones are made from bricks: so old a governor sleeps there in an unmarked grave. Something tells me a youthful Kilgo passed by this ancient burial ground. And then a feathery flash of white flits through the canopy. It couldn't be . . . could it?

We surface on a bluff overlooking the Great Pee Dee River. A snowy egret stalks the shallows on the Marlboro County side. Amid cherrybarks I literally walk in Kilgo's steps. Visions of him in Athens and here merge in a dreamlike way. I sense what a youth among these woods meant to him when he assumed the role of professor. He had to make a reckoning of it, a way to merge two lives. Who we were—and who we become.

Our lives were symmetrical. Kilgo grew up in rural South Carolina and taught and wrote in Georgia. I grew up in rural Georgia and taught and wrote in South Carolina. We were country boys who loved books and the outdoors and found a way to blend both.

I like to think I would earn a higher grade today were I to repeat his course, that we would have much to discuss and much to share after many years of trudging through swamps and dictionaries, but he's gone. Peggy Culbertson is gone, and I have no doubt the dogwood by the window of that classroom window is gone too. I had 54 professors at Georgia. I remember a handful, but I can't forget Kilgo.

Sunday, December 8, 2002, friends sang hymns outside Kilgo's hospital room. He was 61. In 2011 he was posthumously inducted into the Georgia Writers Hall of Fame.

To this day I see the best teacher I ever had. He's wearing a blue-and-white seersucker suit holding a book high as he reads to spellbound students. Faulkner's spiriting us into the woods of Mississippi's fictional Yoknapatawpha County, deep enough to transform the destiny of a student and a man we called Kilgo.

Some things remain the same. Down Mt. Pleasant Way,
Lottie "Winnee" Moultrie Swinton's idea still brings beauty
and function to the Sweetgrass Highway.

PHOTOGRAPH BY ROBERT C. CLARK.

THE ENDURING, ENDEARING SOUTH

The South of old endures here and there and proves endearing to those who appreciate her. Georgialina's free and wild river, the Chattooga, carves a stony border between Georgia and South Carolina just as it did when the Cherokee built fish traps from its rocks. Green milky waters still rush through sieves as they have for 250 million years.

In Georgialina men still stay up all night long turning wires of simmering hogs. Folks are willing to drive 100 miles for down-home barbecue sloshed with sauce. And just smelling hickory coals burning will set your mouth to watering.

In Elbert County, Georgia, Anthony Shoals lives on. Where so many shoals have fallen silent beneath impoundments, this one and its rocky shoals spider lilies narrowly escaped the reach of not one but two dams. It reminds us of the wildness and beauty we sacrifice for hydroelectric power.

If you know where they hide you can still find roads that take you through the South of old. Interesting sights, history, and famous people will greet you along the way. One aspect of the South that remains unchanged is the stately courthouses where justice and political power live. And cherished ways still live along the Sweetgrass Highway and in places with poetic names like Indian Field Camp Ground.

The sweetgrass itself? Well, development is making it hard to find. That old-timey religion? You'll find it when you "go to camp."

The Southland, she lives on in Georgialina, and she lives on in our hearts.

·{ THE CHATTOOGA }·

One river remains wild and free. I rafted it once, and it made a lasting impression. Come, go with me at dawn to shoot Georgialina's wild and scenic river.

It's early morning on this wild river that runs northeast to southwest and cuts deep beneath early daylight. Hurdling downriver between canyon walls, I glide, pitch, jostle, and buck as high above light streams, ricochets, and flares off granite and gneiss walls. Mica fires up and the walls shake with glitter. Asphalt-gray rocks streaked white lean over the river. It's as if an earthquake thrust asphalt highways into airy obtuse angles to remind you of something simple: civilization doesn't exist here.

Here nothing is safe. An ill-fated deer ended up for a week in a keeper hydraulic where it tumbled before the river spat it out, piece by piece.

Upstream, above the Highway 28 bridge, it's much more peaceful. A thick canopy cools the water. Cascades enrich oxygen levels. The romantic fly fisherman at dawn lives here. Standing in riffles arcing casts against a green mountain laurel backdrop, he floats his hand-tied fly upon cool water.

The Cherokee fished all along the river. You can still see their weir in Section IV: structured piles of rocks glistening with purpose long unfulfilled. Sliding sideways upon the current, avoiding boulders, syllable by syllable, I say "Nan-ta-ha-la." This Cherokee word resounds off unforgiving walls. Though I am not on *the* Nantahala, I'm nonetheless in the "Land of the Noonday Sun."

To run the Chattooga in early light is to navigate the edge of night. Rocky cliffs to the west reflect day's first light. All this glancing, dancing light airbrushes the river, giving it an airy, treacherous essence. Geological processes 250 million years old have perfected death traps that have devoured kaleidoscopic kayakers like M&Ms. If you run the Chattooga, you had better be an unerring judge of depths, colors, and shadows.

> I felt as though I had dipped into some supernatural source
> of primal energy. It was like riding on a river of air.
>
> James Dickey, *Deliverance*

Here in fabled Section IV, the Chattooga saves its strongest muscle for its last seven miles, where boulders and ledges beget rapids, sieves, and hydraulics. Entering Seven Foot Falls I'm thrown out as fast as a pencil point breaks midsentence. I toss, tumble, spin, and beat against rocks. I rise against the raft bottom. Once, twice, thrice—inflated air—just what I need holds me underwater. Trapped! On my fourth try, I surface, strangling, and throwing up the Chattooga.

River guide John Michael Wallace, with his 18-inch brown mane and Nazarene beard, looks like Jesus but he can't walk on water. He too goes under at Seven Foot Falls. Wallace likes to run the river in his one-man, inflatable kayak. He's seen the river in all her moods. Seen her quirks, too. He points to shaky spindles of rocks piled atop one another.

"Hippies think those will bring them good luck," he says dryly.

Early light, says Wallace, provides a spectacle on this vestige of wild America. "Oh man, it's amazing. At daybreak, beams shoot above narrow areas, shining onto Georgia trees. When the light strikes the water in wider, open areas, flakes of mica light up. In shallows," Wallace adds as he pushes off a rock, "long flowing trails of algae turn neon green when the light strikes them."

I had seen the trails of fluorescent green pointing downstream. I wasn't sure what I had seen. Light up here is a jester. You see things a drunken friend one night referred to as "one of them optical delusions."

Hard to believe algae cling to anything in this brilliant whitewater, but cling they do. Such tenacity holds a lesson for man, the minor actor in Chattooga dramas.

As we shoot clean between brown rocks, I glimpse the imprint of a fossil in a boulder, a small fish, perhaps, or is it an ancient leaf? Whatever it is, it has been there forever. Me? My name is Sojourner. I am just passing through these canyon walls but what a passage it makes.

And now it's been four days since we shot the Chattooga. Back home I got up early on a Tuesday morning to run at daybreak in Harbison State Forest. At 6:41, the sun popped over the horizon. Yellow light just sifted through green pine tops and then slanted across my front porch.

Early light had one more trick to play. When I put on my shoes, the ones I rafted the Chattooga in, they felt tight, too tight. Talcum-fine river powder had collected in the toe box. I knocked them together and shook 'em good. As I emptied the shoes, shiny mica filled the air with the sparkling light of a Chattooga morning. It hung in still air shimmering, paying gravity no mind.

Suddenly I was back in those splendid hills, the roar of whitewater in my ears, rocks flashing before my eyes. I remembered Seven Foot Falls, and a shiver shot down my spine. It pleased me in some curious way that river glitter was now on my doorsteps and I had seen it one more time.

And it pleases me that this wild river will long run through the enduring, endearing South.

⸺❴ HITE'S DOWN-HOME BBQ ❵⸺

One day when you're starving for traditional pit-cooked BBQ, make your way over to Jackie Hite's Barbecue just off Highway 23 in Leesville, South Carolina. You'll know you're in the right place when you park by the tracks and smell the delicious aroma emanating from hogs sizzling over hickory coals. Look for plumes of smoke back of Hite's wide white restaurant. Inside look for the patriarch of pork, Jackie Hite, who barbecues hogs the old-fashioned, traditional way. Park out front or park to the side.

If you park to the side of Hite's, you'll hear the chop, chop, chop of cleavers and now and then out front the wailing horn of a Northern Suffolk train barreling by. Inside this all-you-can-eat buffet, the clamor of conversation nearly drowns out the wailing train.

Hite's restaurant is open Wednesdays through Sundays, and the crew works through the night cooking hogs. (The process takes about 25 hours.) He gets his hogs, special mustard, and hickory logs from local providers. He burns four-foot logs of hickory in a firebox just outside the pit area. Pitmaster Tim Hyman keeps the path to the pits clean. Back and forth he goes, carrying shovels of red coals, which he spreads beneath sizzling half hogs. A picky type—you know some I'm sure—once asked Hite just how he knew the coals were hot enough. "If them hogs ain't smoking, if them hogs ain't dripping, they ain't cooking," replied Hite, who's been cooking hogs for 42 years. Yep, he knows a thing or two about pork, called by someone the Donald Trump of Barbecue.

He's got a veteran crew that works like a well-greased machine. "I've had the same crew all my life," he says, adding, "Some people just like to work." And some folks—make that a lot of folks—just like to eat his BBQ. Inside the buffet you'll spot locals and visitors from afar. "Folks come here from Alabama to fish and they take my barbecue back to Bama. Georgia too."

Hite takes great pride in the way he cooks pigs. "Sloshing mustard sauce on hogs makes it real BBQ," he says, pulling on the bill of his Gamecock cap. (You won't catch him without that cap.) Now and then he'll pull out a four-foot hickory stick. "Used for two things," he says. "In school for manners and stirring coals in BBQ pits." Hite's a friendly fellow who talks just like he looks, and along with good food he dispenses some life lessons and country wisdom. "I could be a cop without a gun. Folks respect me 'cause I do the right thing." In a way he is a cop without a gun. He's an honorary deputy sheriff and will gladly show you his badge. He'll gladly swap tales with you too.

"Here's how cooking pigs started," he says. "A long time ago a house burned down in China and killed a pig. It smelled so good they started tasting it and then they started cooking hogs. Of course that's an old wife's tale," he says, as a big peal of laughter rolls out.

Before he got in the BBQ business, Jackie Hite, this man who always does the right thing, and his dad ran a hardware store. Jackie tossed his hat in the circle for magistrate once and won. He served just three weeks. His daddy said, "Don't you know you can't be no judge! We got a business to run."

The pull of politics eventually snared him for two terms as mayor. He has plenty of connections. Politicians, judges, policemen, SLED agents, game wardens, lawyers, and others call this garrulous man their friend. He's learned much about life from his BBQ associations. "I got an education and I never went to college," he says, and another mighty roll of laughter escapes.

Today Jackie's business is BBQ, and you can boil his business model down to seven basic words: hogs, hickory, fire, smoke, sauce, and hungry people. As the hogs simmer and Tim rains mustard sauce on them, the smoke rises to the top of the outbuilding and drifts over the community. Says Hite, "Folks drive through and say 'Man yo place smells good!'" Tim covers the simmering hogs with giant sheets of cardboard to keep the smoke in. The cardboard refuses to burn. "We don't throw that kind of heat to it," says Hite. Big 17-quart steel pans filled with barbecued chickens sit on racks. "Three pans will hold two boxes of chickens [26]."

Besides BBQ, Hite's passion is fishing for crappie. As you'd expect, he's most familiar with Clark Hill Lake. "Best fishing is on the Georgia side," he says. "Less development there." He should know. He's a world-class angler with tournament wins, trophies, and photos of fish galore to back him up.

Hite's BBQ is a legend in the Palmetto state. The proof is easy to see. It's a Friday morning. Outside, folks queue up at 10:45, eager to get Hite's BBQ. The line builds as others enter and exit the take-out door, big smiles on their faces. Inside, big vats of cabbage, gravy, rice, skins, green beans, slaw, and more and, of course, BBQ hog and chicken wait for the doors to open. Folks file in and commence to eating. Country girls keep tea glasses full, and a special treat, hot fruit, makes a great dessert, especially if you top it with whipped cream.

Folks, some serious eating goes down here.

A food reviewer wrote that it's worth driving 100 miles to eat at Hite's. Make the trip to Hite's and travel back in time. About $22 will feed two. The buffet opens at 11 o'clock in the morning. Once you get good and full, visit Leesville's Historic College District and Batesburg's Commercial Historic District. Walk around a bit. You'll need to. And know that Jackie Hite, who served as mayor in these parts, put the hyphen between Batesburg and Leesville. "I helped bring these two towns together."

And he'll take care of your longing for traditional, pit-cooked BBQ, expanding your waistline in the process.

·{ ANTHONY SHOALS }·
LIVES ON

Many times Mom spoke of Anthony Shoals as a place prominent in her childhood memories. "It was," she said, "our beach." It's a special place I wanted to see but couldn't. It didn't exist anymore.

As a girl, Mom and her family spent special times there. She remembers quite accurately that the shoals had mountain laurel and rhododendron. They had fish fries and a lot of get-togethers up above the shoals in a place that amounted to a natural campground. Of course there was no electricity, but there was a spring that provided water.

They would pack up live chickens and take everything needed to cook with, lard, staples, and more. Numerous families would be there. Mom said it was where farming families vacationed after they "laid by. They'd take watermelons, cantaloupes . . . mama took a flour sack of homemade biscuits and we'd haul everything there in a wagon pulled by two mules."

They would swim, and what a joy that must have been on a hot summer day. It seems rustic now, but, looking back, that's how life was. It's romantic in the sense that it serves up an idealized view of a difficult time. It was a time when most of the creature comforts we take for granted didn't exist, and that, too, further underscores what a special place Anthony Shoals was. It was in a real way an oasis. A "beach-like" adventure—only I find it better than today's beaches.

I myself have memories of the place. I remember a fish fry I went to there as a boy. Three things stand out from that day—the beautiful rock-studded waters, the feeling that this place was special, and how a man scoured a frying pan with river sand until it shone like a mirror. Oddly, I have no memory of eating fried fish that day.

All my life I assumed the entire shoals were beneath Clark Hill Lake, and that confused me because I did some math and found I should have been too young to remember the place. Still, I had this memory of a place that I didn't think existed, and I just couldn't square things in my mind. Clark Hill Dam was completed in 1954, and surely the waters had covered Anthony Shoals, but, no, I was mistaken.

Sometimes it's great to be wrong. Anthony Shoals still exists. In fact, it's part of the Broad River Wildlife Management Area. You'll find rapids at Anthony Shoals, a very long series of rapids of Class II difficulty. You'll also find a channel cut through ledges so that barges from yesteryear could travel upstream. Canoeists and kayakers love the shoals.

What's not to love? Grassy islets, forest-clad slopes, and a rocky streambed hosting rushing water make a picturesque setting. And it gets even prettier come spring. Anthony Shoals is the only place on the Broad River that supports the rare rocky shoals spider lilies that dwell on Southeast fall-line rivers. History lives here, too. The area harbors remnants from previous settlements, including Native American mounds and the ruins of old mills and factories from the 1700s.

In researching Anthony Shoals, I ran across stunning paintings by an Augusta native, Philip Juras. Philip, who lives in Athens, focuses on remnant natural landscapes that offer a glimpse of the Southeast before European settlement changed so many things.

Here's an excerpt from Philip's essay in *Bartram's Living Legacy: Travels and the Nature of the South*:

> There is no river scene in the Piedmont of northeast Georgia more stunning than Anthony Shoals on the Broad River. Perhaps there used to be. Perhaps the many great shoals on the Savannah River were just as glorious before they fell silent beneath the waters of the Thurmond, Russell, and Hartwell reservoirs, but I'm not quite old enough to have known any of them. Only the rapids above Augusta, my hometown, still show the

beauty of the Savannah before it leaves the Piedmont. But the wildness of the river there is diminished by the new mansions looking down from the bluffs and the dams parceling out the flow from upstream. I think that's why I love Anthony Shoals so much. This final stretch of the Broad, as it runs through the Broad River Wildlife Management Area, is the only place in the upper Savannah River watershed where the sound of a wild river still rises from such a wide swath of bedrock.

Juras continues commenting on the setting for his splendid painting: "On the evening I captured this view, mountain laurel, snowbells, mock orange, Piedmont rhododendron, and fringe tree were in various states of bloom on the steep slopes next to the river. The main show, however, was being staged on the river itself, where one of the few populations of shoals spider lilies left in the Savannah watershed was catching the light of the western horizon with glorious full blooms."

Juras recounts how Anthony Shoals avoided being dammed by two proposed hydropower dams. "Though spared in the 20th century, the shoals have certainly seen human activity before then. If this view had been painted 150 years ago, the Broad River Manufacturing Company would appear on the opposite bank. Its millrace would be visible reaching upstream to the head of the shoals, and in that view much of the forest would have been cleared from the hills. However, if you imagine an earlier time when Native Americans inhabited this area, it's likely the scene would appear much as it does today."

Like Mom, like Juras, I find Anthony Shoals fascinating. I plan to go there soon with my camera and laptop. I'll find a shady spot with a command of the shoals and reflect on all that's transpired here. I'll imagine Native Americans gazing at the rare shoals lilies of spring. I'll watch barges poled and dragged upstream with cargoes destined for merchants in the Piedmont. I'll see whitewater rushing through the distant mill's millrace delivering the most natural power imaginable. I'll watch kids playing as their parents prepare a tremendous picnic. I'll see an artist painting his beautiful landscapes. Best of all, I'll take solace in rediscovering a place from childhood, one I thought lay beneath lake waters like so many other long-lost treasures.

The shoals, by the way, take their name from relatives on my mom's side of the family. That's where my daughter, Becky, gets hers middle name: Rebecca Anthony Korom.

And now I discover that people actually pursue rock climbing there on a small group of challenging boulders, several of which have "climbable problems."

I can't wait to go there. I'll spend an afternoon at a place where my mom spent some of her more memorable childhood days, a jewel of a place that still sparkles. In the most vivid sense imaginable, I'll time-travel to a place I long thought humankind had destroyed.

·{ THE OLD }·
{ SOUTH }

There's an old road in South Carolina that makes for a great Sunday drive. You can see historic sites, get the feeling you are in the mountains, and yet feel you are at the coast, all at the same time. You'll come across the ghosts of historic characters, too.

Old S.C. State Route 261, birthed by an Indian path, became the Great Charleston Road. Rich with old churches and plantations, this passage hosted a Civil War diarist, governors, and Revolutionary and Confederate generals, and just off its path rests a man we should think of come Christmas.

A historical marker at Route 261's junction with Highway 378 greets travelers, saying, "Over it came Indians, pack animals laden with hides, drovers, rolled hogsheads of produce, wagoners, and stagecoaches. The armies of two wars passed over it."

Some called it the King's Highway, and it barely missed being a thoroughfare to the state capital. In the 1780s the South Carolina General Assembly decided to move the state capital from Charleston to the state's central region. Stateburg lost by a handful of votes to Granby, which Columbia eclipsed in time.

Today, as then, State Route 261 winds through the High Hills of Santee. This area is rural, isolated, and heartbreakingly antebellum. Here and there the land plunges, opening up vistas of distant ridges. You think at once of the mountains. It's a curious sight to see Spanish moss in the mountains, but that's what Highway 261 gives you in the High Hills: massive oaks with limbs trailing draperies of Spanish moss. The coast is far, far away, and yet the oaks here assume a feathery persona . . . they look like bird wings and maybe they should, for there's a rare breed of artist here in the High Hills of Santee.

In the Stateburg Historic District alone, you'll find enough history to fill several good-size books. For starters there's the Church of the Holy Cross. This stately old church was built from 1850 to 1852 of rammed earth, the product of a technique for building walls that compacts earth, chalk, lime, and gravel into concrete-like hardness.

In its beautiful old cemetery lies Joel Roberts Poinsett, the man who brought us the poinsettia. He was a botanist, physician, and statesman who served in the U.S. House of Representatives and who was the first U.S. minister to Mexico. It was there that he saw the noche buena, the red-leaved plant that would carry his name.

Across the road from the church you'll find the Borough House Plantation. This beautiful home was destined to share ties with warring generals. The original home, built in 1758, served as the headquarters for the British general Lord Cornwallis and the American general Nathanael Greene during the Revolutionary War . . . at different times, of course. The second house, built here in 1820, was the birthplace of Confederate general Richard H. Anderson. His father was Dr. William Wallace Anderson. Joel Poinsett, by the way, came to pay Dr. Anderson a visit, and while there he died. Thus did he end up in the cemetery across Highway 261.

Just a ways down the road and a bit off the beaten path you'll come across the grave of General Thomas Sumter, the "Carolina Gamecock." He earned his nickname after a rampage during which he killed British soldiers for burning down his house.

Those of you who recall Ken Burns's *Civil War* documentary will recognize the name Mary Boykin Chestnut. She grew up in Stateburg, a stone's throw from Route 261. Mary Boykin Chestnut published her Civil War diary as a "vivid picture of a society in the throes of its life-and-death struggle."

Today Grainger McKoy, a noted wildlife sculptor, lives in Boykin's childhood home. McKoy has xylem for blood vessels. Working with wood has driven his art from childhood on.

"As a young child, I marveled at my father notching cypress logs, as the cabin in which I grew up in took shape." An old decoy his grandmother gave him moved something deep inside him. His mother held him up by his belt so that he could saw an exterior log end from that cypress cabin. From that log end he sculpted his first bird in 1960. That's when he "peered over the edge of the nest into the world of sculpture," as he puts it. All that family support played a prominent role in his art. "Your true inheritance," he says, "is what's left that you can't spend."

Whereas other sculptors portrayed a bird sitting inertly, McKoy gave his life-like action. McKoy's sculptures of a bobwhite covey rise and sanderlings in flight "defy belief as well as gravity." To see his Carolina parakeets in flight is to see an extinct species spring to life.

"April" William Ellison Jr. also owned the house McKoy lives in. A free man and former slave, Ellison achieved success as a cotton gin maker and blacksmith prior to the Civil War. He became a major planter and one of the state's largest property owners. At his death Ellison held 60 slaves and more than 1,000 acres of land.

Just down the road you'll find the hamlet of Boykin Mill Pond. There you'll see a quaint old church, Swift Creek Church. Floods of tears fell onto its pews and heart-pine floors. In May 1860 approximately 75 young people met on a Saturday at Boykin Mill pond to picnic right near the church. Late that afternoon 30 or more crowded onto a flatboat, and it overturned. Those who could swim tried to save the lives of those who could not, but close to 25 young people drowned, mostly women.

You'll find an old mill here, too. Boykin Mill and its 100-year-old turbines keep rolling on, preserving a time when mills provided nearby communities with cornmeal, grits, and flour.

There's a lot more to Route 261 and Stateburg. If you want to take an interesting trip, drive the old King's Highway. The sheer isolation will give you the feeling you are in the 1850s. The only thing that breaks the spell is a golf course just off the old road.

As I drove along the winding oak-shaded lane, I avoided looking at the golf course. I was envisioning other things, things from our past. I conjured up a horse and buggy with men in powdered wigs and women in colonial attire. I added some Redcoats with muskets, and that scene was complete. Then that scene gave way to a regiment of Confederates marching down the road, the dust rising and hanging in the air. The men are tired, tattered, and dejected. Visiting her childhood home and looking out the upstairs window, Mary Boykin Chestnut sees the men and reaches for her diary as all, one by one, vanish into the eternal mists we call history.

.{ THE SEAT OF }. POWER

Law-abiding Georgians love their courthouses, and well they should. Georgia has one of America's great collections of courthouses. The buildings' architecture ranges from Greek Revival to International Style. In fact, just about every architectural style imaginable can be found in Georgia's 159 counties.

What's interesting is that although Georgia is the twentieth largest state, it is second in number of courthouses. Only Texas has more. Without doubt, Georgia has a reputation for having some of the more beautiful and historic courthouses in the country.

In the smaller, rural counties, the courthouse reigns as the area's indisputable architectural gem. It's the county's ultimate power symbol, too: the incontestable seat of power. Few structures provide a more powerful focal point for good behavior than the courthouse.

I traveled to many towns while working on a book about the history of worker's compensation insurance in Georgia. I interviewed a lot of lawyers, and, not surprisingly, I visited a lot of courthouses. Most are gems. Just about all of them serve as imposing reminders of where true power resides. One hundred thirty-two Georgia courthouses are listed in the National Register of Historic Places. Lincoln County's courthouse stands among them.

We came by today's courthouse in a series of phases. When legislation carved Lincoln County from Wilkes County in 1796, the act stipulated that county commissioners select a site for a county seat and build a courthouse there. The 1796 act further directed that elections and court sessions first be held at Joseph Stovall's house.

Lincolnton, settled near a spring then called Founders Spring, was named the county seat around 1800. The first court in Lincoln County was held in the old Ferguson House, which afterwards became the Dozier Hotel. When Lincolnton was designated the county seat, a stone courthouse was built. Later, on March 2, 1874, the legislature approved Lincoln County's loan of $12,000 for building a new courthouse. That two-story courthouse rose from Lincoln County soil and served the people until 1915, when the present courthouse was built. An architectural website states that Little, Cleckler Construction Company built the current brick and stone structure and that the architect G. Lloyd Preacher designed the building. The cost of construction for building the Neoclassical Revival courthouse was $24,340.

Neoclassical Revival architecture is "defined by a commanding facade with a full height porch, its roof supported by classical columns. The columns are often fluted and the capitals are usually ornate Ionic or Corinthian. The Neoclassical Revival is also symmetrical with its entry centered and flanked by a balanced array of windows. Curved, flat roofed porticos are seen occasionally" (http://www.antiquehome style.com).

The Neoclassical Revival style has been prominently used for public buildings and banks, institutions where people anticipate a bit of gravitas or dignity. Getting divorced, filing a deed, and condemning a man to the gallows quite rightly deserve a degree of solemnity. It wouldn't seem as judicial, would it, to receive a life sentence while standing before a judge in a mobile home?

As you'd expect, being the seat of power, county courthouses see their share of drama and life-changing decisions. Thus the courthouse plays a prominent role in Southern literature. Take Harper Lee's *To Kill a Mockingbird*. Hollywood went to great pains to re-create the courtroom for Atticus Finch in the Monroe County, Alabama, courthouse for the film version of *To Kill a Mockingbird*. And that most Southern of writers, William Faulkner, referred to this omnipresent symbol of power in *Requiem for a Nun*, using grandiose words: "But above all, the courthouse: the center, the focus, the hub; sitting looming in the center of the county's circumference like a single cloud in its ring of horizon, laying its vast shadow to the uttermost rim of horizon; musing, brooding, symbolic and ponderable, tall as cloud, solid as rock, dominating all: protector of the weak, judiciate and curb of the passions and lusts, repository and guardian of the aspirations and the hopes."

For certain, courthouses serve up a mix of stories, plots, and memories.

When I was a boy, the courthouse impressed me, intimidated me even. First of all, I found its size to be mammoth. It was the only building in Lincolnton visible from three miles away on the Augusta Highway where I grew up. Even now, driving toward Lincolnton, if you know just where and when to look, the courthouse reveals itself on the horizon. You'll see the courthouse dome peek over the green tree line.

Second, the place struck me as the site for serious matters. As a boy, whenever I entered the building I got the notion that I was in a sacred, powerful place. I knew it was the last stop a fellow would make before landing in jail.

My friend and teammate Eddie Drinkard remembers fondly when Vern Sturkey, the custodian/janitor, would take several kids up into the clock tower. "We'd go up some stairs in the dark. There was a small square that would open so you could see out above the houses and trees. There was always one condition, we had to be out before the next time the clock struck. It would burst your eardrums or so we were told and we were not taking any chances."

That experience, said Eddie, was pretty cool when you were seven to eight years old. "Also," he said, "if you were lucky enough to have a pair of roller skates (the metal kind with a key to tighten it onto the soles of your shoes) we would skate on the concrete around the monument in front of the courthouse. Sort of a 1960s version of Roller Derby!"

"Going into the courtroom." That phrase has a negative tone to it if you are on the wrong side of the law. But that's why such buildings exist: to dispense justice, sort out disputes, maintain records, and in general bring an orderly way of life to the people in the county. And, you could say with authenticity, to add an element of beauty as well.

Atop Lincoln County's courthouse, one more than 100 years old, sits a cupola with a green patina like that of oxidized copper. Green metal roofing matches the cupola. The deep red bricks contrast with the four white columns. Those red bricks came from Lincoln County clay. Out front fly the state and national flags. Between those flags stands the county's memorial to local veterans of four wars who made the supreme sacrifice. Those men fought that we can be free, that we have the right to make laws and see that justice is served. They died so that you can use the courthouse and judicial system to redress grievances and wrongs.

Thus do we have courthouses all over Georgia. These grand old buildings house the scales of justice, which generally do their thing in a just and impartial manner. On the absolute top of our courthouse you'll find a weathervane. "Justice is often the wind that blows the criminal to his punishment" goes the old quote. This stately old courthouse has long blown justice to criminals while doing its share to contribute to Georgia's legacy as a state known for its alluring seats of power. Beauty, history, justice, social conventions, and architecture: they all come together and reside at the courthouse.

·⟩ DOWN BY THE ⟨· SWEETGRASS HIGHWAY

I was a boy when I first saw Mount Pleasant's sweetgrass basket weavers. My aunt and uncle lived in Summerville, where I spent two weeks each summer. Often we went to Mount Pleasant. Shooting across the Cooper River Bridge, we arrived in a countryside peopled by weavers. Wearing white dresses and white hats with wide brims, they looked like a Jonathan Green painting.

"What are they doing?"

"Making sweetgrass baskets," said my aunt.

Now sweetgrass to me was a grass Mom introduced me to in Georgia. Pull a tender handful to your face and you'd smell the sweetest incense. The ladies along the highway, I would learn, were weaving a tougher kind of sweetgrass, and in time their classic baskets would give a seven-mile stretch of highway a name.

The ladies sat far off the road patiently weaving, waiting for buyers. Highway 17 was a two-lane highway back then with generous grassy shoulders. The daughters and granddaughters of the women I saw as a boy carry on the tradition, but Highway 17 today is a six-lane highway heavy with traffic. Restaurants and a brick mall sprawl along its right of way. Snarling mufflers, blaring horns, and whining tires destroy serenity.

Sirens bring an ominous sound to the mix. Cement mixers, 18-wheelers, buses, and cars fly by mere feet from the women. Catastrophe is one blown tire, one text away. Medals should honor these courageous women, who are as much a part of the lowcountry as she-crab soup, live oaks, and sea oats. A princely sum will buy you a basket, but if you think $1,195 for a hand-woven basket is too much, hold on. There's much to know about all that goes into it. Let's start with the baskets' rich history.

Weaving sweetgrass baskets is an American art with African origins. When slaves came to South Carolina from Sierra Leone, they brought basket-making skills. They made baskets from bulrush, white oak, and saw palmetto, and rice plantations found many uses for them.

Sweetgrass grew in popularity when women in Mount Pleasant began making "show baskets" for tourists along Route 17. The 1929 opening of the Grace Bridge that connected Charleston to Mount Pleasant gave Lottie "Winnee" Moultrie Swinton an idea. She decided to sit in a chair with her baskets along Highway 17. People pulled onto the shoulder, and a tradition was born. Today the stretch of Highway 17 near Mount Pleasant is officially designated the Sweetgrass Basket Makers Highway. Up and down the road, on both sides, ladies sit, weave, and sell their wares.

The highway needs them. Any charm the highway has today comes from the women, but there wouldn't be much time for making baskets if weavers gathered their own grass. Men harvest *Muhlenbergia filipes*, purple muhly grass. They slip the grass from its roots and dry it in the sun. Once it's cut into sheaves, they sell it to the weavers, who work it into coils.

Most folks fail to notice this ordinary-looking plant much of the year, but come autumn its vibrant pinkish-purple plumes are unmistakable. When the setting sun backlights this long-stemmed rosy-pink plant, it blazes as if afire.

"Grass getting so hard to find," says Elizabeth Eady. "The guys have to go so far sometimes." She focuses on her hands as they work a spoon handle and grass. The faces of some people reveal the cumulative wisdom of years. Elizabeth is such a person. She's been weaving baskets all her life. She can't estimate how many baskets she's made. As she coils grass, she says in a matter-of-fact way, "Made my first piece before I went to the first grade."

She uses simple implements just as her predecessors did—forks and spoons. "Break those handles off, file 'em down, and start weaving."

Elizabeth and her sister Mabel (Elizabeth calls her May) sit in a stand just off 17's inbound lanes to Mount Pleasant. Their voices are soft, their words measured as if they're timing them to their stitches. A green and white cement truck barrels by, and the plastic nailed to their stand flaps and rattles. Come winter the plastic will keep the wind out, but it doesn't mute traffic, nor is it any protection from out-of-control drivers.

"Do you worry about getting hit by a truck?" I shout to Mabel.

"Every hour of every day," she says.

The women work from 8:30 to 6:30 seven days a week, weather permitting. When they arrive, they unpack their baskets and hang them on nails jutting from the two by fours that frame their stand. Stand downwind of those baskets and you'll think you're in a hay field. "When you clean the baskets it makes the smell fresh," says Elizabeth. "They'll smell that way all their life."

Mabel works on a small basket. "How long does it take to make a basket like that?" I ask. (A day maybe?) A musical laugh like wind chimes escapes Mabel, a shy lady according to Elizabeth. "I'm on my third day. I've got five more rows to go, so I'll have four days in this basket." Four days of sitting by this murderer's row of traffic. "You get used to it," says Elizabeth.

Weaving baskets is so hard it'll make you cuss.
Damn, this is hard.
Elizabeth Eady

"You saw my mother and aunt," says Elizabeth. I had just told the ladies about seeing weavers in the early 1960s. "If you saw weavers you saw them." Their aunt, Katherine Cooper Johnson, taught them to weave. She was a perfectionist. "If I made a mistake my aunt would take the whole thing apart and I'd have to start all over," says Elizabeth.

"Getting a basket started is the hardest part," says Mabel.

"Weaving baskets is so hard it'll make you cuss," says Elizabeth. "Damn, this is hard." To this day the women start over if they make a mistake. Once a basket is off to a good start it becomes a matter of patience, skill, and technique passed from generation to generation. Slowly a work of art forms whose symmetry, precision, and colors give sweetgrass baskets their classic appearance. "Longleaf pine needles give the baskets their brown rings. We add bulrush, too," says Mabel.

A cell phone rings, out of place among the baskets and sheaves of grass. Elizabeth announces that she has to leave early to go to church, where she works part time. I offer to help her load her baskets, but she declines.

"Thank you, but they have to be packed just so."

Basket making itself remains as it was when it came from West Africa. The biggest and worst changes come from modern life. Gated communities choke off access to the grass, and widened highways and development squeeze the women into a narrow zone. That thin line running from stall to stall along Highway 17? Call it the twilight zone. Basket weaving could be approaching its twilight. The weavers are dying, and grass is harder than ever to get. Still, a glimmer of hope flickers. "A lot more young people are into weaving," says Mabel.

That's good. We need weavers. Their baskets, born of loving labor, remind us of those days long ago when form gave function a beautiful way to accomplish tasks. Separate that chaff . . . hold those vegetables . . . carry those shellfish.

And what can be said about Elizabeth and Mabel? Well, they've worked all their lives making baskets down by the Sweetgrass Highway just two miles from Hamlin Road where they grew up. In an era when people jump all over the country like cash-crazy crickets, these sisters have stayed the course, living and working just as their predecessors did. Life wouldn't be as beautiful without them, nor would the Sweetgrass Highway's name ring true.

·{ WE'RE GOING }·
{ TO CAMP }

I had heard such places existed. Now I was just two miles from seeing one. Just off I-26 near Ridgeville, South Carolina, I began to see signs. I followed them, took a side road, and the place came into view. Time for a deep breath. Old photographs of Nazi concentration camps came to mind. It was an illusion, of course, created by the way the old cabins sit shoulder to shoulder. Dark clapboards, rusty tin roofs, and stark chimneys strengthened the impression.

How ironic that this soul-saving place reminded me of a concentration camp. But it's just an illusion, for the Cypress Methodist Camp Ground is where old-time religion is alive and well. Georgia's got some campgrounds, too. One is near Cumming, the Holbrook Campground. For 175 years people have been meeting at Holbrook, where they can get "some of that old time religion and it is the next thing to Heaven on this earth" (http://www.holbrookcampmeeting .com).

The Marietta Camp Ground has had an annual camp meeting since 1837. In the old days, for months before camp, "Tenters were busy preparing for camp meeting. In the early days, spinning and weaving and making cloth into garments consumed much time, for there were no sewing machines and all this was done by hand. Water buckets were of cedar, many of them homemade. They were scoured with soap and sand until they were bright and the brass hoops looked like gold." All campgrounds have such histories and tons of hard work behind the scenes.

The Cypress Methodist Camp Ground, one of a few campgrounds in South Carolina, continues to host annual weeklong camp meetings. Georgia's and South Carolina's annual gatherings are a carryover from the Great Awakening in American religious life that swept through the American colonies in the 1730s and 1740s. The Awakening led people to "new birth," inspired by the preaching of the Word.

The afternoon was steamy, and there I was on Holy Ground in the lowcountry down Jedburg way. As I drove up and glanced at the Cypress Methodist Camp Ground, it looked too like a shantytown, though, of course, it isn't. Cypress Camp Ground, I'll shorten it, has a beauty all its own, and it's no flash in the pan. Folks have been gathering here to sing, pray, and hear the gospel for 219 years. Families own the tents, and specific guidelines determine how they are passed down. It's an heirloom.

I parked beneath a big oak dripping Spanish moss and walked the grounds, trying to imagine what a meeting must have been like in the old days. Had to be full of sounds, sights, and sensations. Gospel songs ringing out. Maybe an old foot-pedal organ, too. Greens and sweet potatoes cooking. Lots of good conversation. For sure, far-flung families looked forward to a bit of a reunion. Kids played and laughed while old folks caught up. And at day's end they "camped" in the rough-hewn tents.

Calling the rough-hewn wood cabins "tents" is a carryover from the days when people slept in canvas tents. These cabins, roughly rectangular, are generally 1.5 stories with earthen floors. A small stairway or ladder leads to the upper story.

In the center of the rectangle stands the tabernacle, an open-sided wooden structure. It looks a lot like a shelter in a state park. Its pews, washed by rains blowing in, are weathered and worn smooth by many a rear.

Across the lane running alongside the campground stands a row of around a dozen privies. They look like an old-fashioned version of the portalets we see at football games and festivals. The old wooden outhouses possess more class by far. The door of one outhouse stood open, as if someone had just paid it a visit. A vine hung from the ceiling like Christmas garland. Some were padlocked, and two had wildflowers blooming yellow in front. Using one with a neighbor perched next door requires a bit of courage, I'd imagine. The people come, though, and use them they do.

Five communities support this campground: Givhans, Lebanon, New Hope, Ridgeville, and Zion. Serving crowds too large for church buildings or homes, the campground responded to religious and social needs. Some campgrounds provided courtship opportunities. Of one campground Charleston's *Post and Courier* reported, "It says a lot of what you need to know about Camp Meeting that it's always been and still is a place of courtship. The meetings are open to the public. An invitation into a family tent is considered a cachet."

The tents allowed people to stay overnight, and the "campground" term remained even though rough-hewn cabins gradually replaced the tents. Cypress Camp Ground opened in 1794, and an adjacent cemetery contains graves from the early 1800s. This old campground is on the National Register of Historic Places. And deservedly so.

A friend's family owns a tent at Indian Fields Campground, near St. George. "If you want to spend the night," Carol said, "you may have to come during the week to get a bed. And you won't get much sleep, so think about this. It is definitely an experience!"

You'll find Cattle Creek Campground near Rowesville. Still other campgrounds are off the beaten path, but you seldom hear of these throwbacks to the days when folks would live and pray together a week at a time.

That old-time religion. It's rural, it's passionate, and it carries on. Then as now it was a time for the Lord and a time for family. It was a time to stand over the graves of loved ones. More often than not, it was hot and sometimes cold. The winds cut right through the boards. Sleep did not come many nights, but each morning broke with hope in the air.

"We're going to camp."

Those words carry the weight of well over 200 years. Folks don't need plumbing, televisions, or air-conditioning. Just that old-time religion. It's good enough for them.

Every child remembers the first arrowhead. . . .
It was better than unearthing diamonds and gold.

PHOTOGRAPH BY ROBERT C. CLARK.

AFTERWORD
The Old Home Place

Much of what's in *Georgialina: A Southland as We Knew It* took root in the home of my maternal grandparents, a Southern home if ever there was. Sadly, each year, Georgialina's boundaries retreat. In 1995, I was talking with James Dickey about the loss of things Southern, and he deplored "the industrial culture and the industrial civilization that had encroached on the Southern pastoral and agrarian way of life." He called this intrusion "the Leviathan—the all-devouring beast of the Bible."

Dickey knew the Southern Agrarians, known also as the Fugitives. Twelve men, among them Robert Penn Warren, Andrew Lytle, John Crowe Ransom, and Donald Davidson, long ago confronted the changes modern life, urbanism, and industrialism brought to Southern culture and traditions.

"They didn't want change," said Dickey. "They wanted to keep the farming economy down here and the connection to the land and not industrialize and not allow or encourage mercantilism, industrialism. The men lost, but they stated the case."

A lot of folks lost. A woman wrote me about her aunt and uncle's old farmhouse. "When I was a child, my uncle and aunt had a dairy farm in Anderson, South Carolina. The home was a huge white house with a screened porch on two sides where we would run around. The house was right next to the dairy; a barbed wire fence kept the cows out of the yard."

When her aunt and uncle passed away, the house was torn down and a Singer sewing machine plant sprung up where cows once grazed. Well, the Leviathan didn't get Mom's home place, a place the Fugitives would have loved. A great deal of *Georgialina: A Southland as We Knew It* sprung from my boyhood experiences at her childhood home.

Just before completing this book, on a May day when the trees were so green they could blind you, I drove to where Mom grew up. I wanted to see if golden profusions of jonquils still bunched up in their beautiful disorderly way. Going there would be bittersweet. The home burned to the ground in 1964. All the laughter and love that lived there were no more. The family members that gathered there—close to 50—number nine now.

My grandparent's tin-roofed home sat just off the Elberton Highway, about three miles west of the South Carolina line as the crow flies. It was a handsome home with a symmetrical architecture whose style eludes me. It was white, wooden, had two chimneys, a front porch with six simple columns, and a screened porch in the back. Later, when I was all grown and a writer, the vicinity surrounding that home, I discovered, had outfitted me with great stories and a sense of place.

As I drove to the old home place, I passed the Chennault Place, where the Confederate gold train was robbed, and then the road to Danburg before arriving at Mom's old community, Beulah. Passing Beulah Baptist Church, I glanced over to where my grandparents lie in rest. Just beyond the church I rounded a long, sweeping curve. Down on the right, the old home place had surrendered to woods. Nature had quietly used a half-century to reclaim what was hers.

A steel cattle gate and heavy cables barred entrance to the driveway that grass, weeds, and trees had long overtaken. Atop the gate was a black and red plastic sign: "Absolutely No Trespassing." The home place no longer belongs to the family. Sold long ago. I eased between two strands of cable and trespassed into my childhood.

Granddad's old store, its asbestos shingles covered by tin, still stood. About 100 paces to the northeast was the old well where I once cranked a windlass to haul up buckets of water. We'd sip water from a newfangled aluminum ladle. A fiberglass well house covered the well. Progress.

All these years later, no trees had claimed the space, a show of respect of some mighty and natural kind as far as I'm concerned. The chimneys and rock columns were gone. Bulldozed and hauled off by the new owner. A fine cover of vetch covered the ground where the old home had stood. In the air some three to four feet above that square of vetch is where I spent many a boyhood day and night. Up front and center, at the front door next to a picture of Gainsborough's *The Blue Boy*, Uncle Carroll, who could never catch a break, told me how men used an old crank telephone to catch fish. Near the old stove a few feet away, Uncle Donald had shown me a shard of aluminum he'd scavenged from a fighter jet that had crashed nearby in the 1950s. Holding it felt magical, powerful, but scary, too. What had happened to the pilot? And it was in the front bedroom to the right where I slept between thick quilts on a feather mattress winter nights.

Behind me once stood a mighty oak. Granddad would tie a giant stalk of bamboo 60 feet tall against it. That bamboo was as tall as the Empire State Building. With a wire running its length, it served as a super antenna for his old radio. I want to say he listened to the Grand Old Opry via that wire, but I just don't know.

Just beyond the well stood the smokehouse. It was a dark, sweet-smelling place where, peeking through cracks, I could see motes of dust floating in shafts of sunlight. A crabapple tree stood to the right of the smokehouse and, far to the right of it, the outhouse, the first one I used. There, my cousins Larry and Ronnie and I, miscreants all, poked girls in their rear with long cane poles we commandeered with our pocketknives. Shrieking and screaming, they bolted from the double-seater.

As I looked around, other memories flooded over me. I found my first arrowhead in a nearby field. Holding that spear point, to be precise, was more exciting than winning a lottery. Here, above the vetch, Grandmom Walker showed me her Indian-head pennies and Indian doll faces she'd found as a girl. I shot my cousins with the peashooters I cut from the lush bamboo on the property. (Bamboo was the only grass allowed, and "allowed" is being kind. Mom says they fought it like the dickens.) My grandparents swept their yard, and buried in that clean, sandy soil was an old millstone, one half protruding above ground—a small arch of granite.

Come summer, Granddad fashioned a lattice of hemp and grew kudzu across his front porch, a green shield against the western sun. Not far away rippled and riffled Anthony Shoals, the place where mom and her family vacationed after getting the crops in. Mom said it was where farming families vacationed after they "laid by." They'd take watermelons, cantaloupes, a flour sack of homemade biscuits, and live chickens to be slaughtered and fried. They hauled everything there in a wagon pulled by two mules.

Come winter evenings, we grandkids shivered with fear around the old wood stove to listen to our great-aunt's stories about the "white thing," a large white panther that spooked the men's horses. We heard stories, too, about the drowned ghost towns of Lisbon and Petersburg. During the telling, a cousin would sneak off to use the jar beneath a bed in the back bedroom. The home had no plumbing and, something even better, no TV. Stories were all we needed.

Walking through the vetch, I resurrected more memories. How fun it was to see the colored candies in Granddad's store and, when no one was looking, snatch a handful of Mary Janes. Near Granddad's minnow tank grew a yucca. My cousins and I would slice off the sharp-pointed leaves with our Barlow pocketknives and spear minnows. Had he caught us, I probably wouldn't be here today. Times were tough, and he needed every penny he could make.

Walking around, I could find no artifacts from the old home place. Even the old millstone was gone. Granddad had relocated it to his new home across the road and painted it red, white, and blue. Many years ago I had scavenged a white enamel pot from underbrush and given it to Mom, a memorial of sorts. The new owner carted all remnants of life off. Only memories remain.

In the end, we borrow places for a while, and that had been the case with Grandfather Walker's place. Nature has it now, not the Leviathan, and for that I'm grateful. The isolation of northern Lincoln County saved it. Mostly deer hunters and fishermen frequent the region. Businessmen and developers leave it be, as they say in these parts. No money to be had.

As for the uninformed who round that big, sweeping curve and head downhill to the free-running remnant of the Broad River, well, they know nothing of the history of the land to their right. That history and others like it are disappearing all across Georgialina. Some of us must record it. It makes for a beautiful burden.

When I was a boy, I had no way of knowing of just how Mom's old home would affect me. Maybe it's had an effect on you, too. Whether it has or not, I hope your journey through *Georgialina: A Southland as We Knew It,* renews your sense of place and appreciation for the old ways. Cherish today, but never forget the past. It helped make us who we are.

2015

12/15/18   3x